SCHOOLING FOR DEMOCRACY IN A TIME OF GLOBAL CRISIS

Schooling for Democracy in a Time of Global Crisis combines democratic theory with education practice to address the problem of a schooling that is *for* democracy, and points to the possibilities, limits and tensions of attempting to re-imagine education in more inclusive, collective and sustainable ways through democratic action.

Contemporary liberal–democratic societies are faced with multiple complex global crises, which demand a range of responses, including how education can produce critical and engaged young people with a collective commitment to tackling the effects of the global climate crisis, growing social and economic inequalities, political instability, insecurity, fear and hate. This book examines how more critically democratic educational policies and practices, and the daily actions of learners, educators, leaders, communities and societies can work towards collective well-being, increased civic participation and commitment to an ecologically sustainable engagement with the planet.

In addition to being a work of critical scholarly analysis, this book provides a manifesto for the possibilities of contemporary democratic education in a time of global crisis. This book will be of great interest to researchers, postgraduate students and policymakers in education.

Stewart Riddle is an Associate Professor in the School of Education at the University of Southern Queensland. His research examines the democratisation of schooling systems, increasing access and equity in education and how schooling can respond to critical social issues in complex contemporary times.

SCHOOLING FOR DEMOCRACY IN A TIME OF GLOBAL CRISIS

Towards a More Caring, Inclusive and Sustainable Future

Stewart Riddle

LONDON AND NEW YORK

Cover image: © Getty Images
First published 2022

by Routledge
4 Park Square, Milton Park, Abingdon, Oxon OX14 4RN

and by Routledge
605 Third Avenue, New York, NY 10158

Routledge is an imprint of the Taylor & Francis Group, an informa business

© 2022 Stewart Riddle

The right of Stewart Riddle to be identified as author of this work has been asserted in accordance with sections 77 and 78 of the Copyright, Designs and Patents Act 1988.

All rights reserved. No part of this book may be reprinted or reproduced or utilised in any form or by any electronic, mechanical, or other means, now known or hereafter invented, including photocopying and recording, or in any information storage or retrieval system, without permission in writing from the publishers.

Trademark notice: Product or corporate names may be trademarks or registered trademarks, and are used only for identification and explanation without intent to infringe.

British Library Cataloguing-in-Publication Data
A catalogue record for this book is available from the British Library

Library of Congress Cataloging-in-Publication Data
Names: Riddle, Stewart, author.
Title: Schooling for democracy in a time of global crisis : towards a more caring, inclusive and sustainable future / Stewart Riddle.
Description: Abingdon, Oxon ; New York, NY : Routledge, 2022. | Includes bibliographical references and index. | Contents: Living and learning in an age of global crisis – Is this the end of the democratic dream? – Pandemics and populism in a post-truth world – A self-made climate catastrophe – Propositions for democratic schooling. |
Identifiers: LCCN 2021052391 | ISBN 9780367636371 (hardback) | ISBN 9780367636425 (paperback) | ISBN 9781003120063 (ebook)
Subjects: LCSH: Democracy and education. | Education and state. | Sustainability–Study and teaching. | Education–Political aspects.
Classification: LCC LC71 .R48 2022 | DDC 370.11/5–dc23/ eng/20211116
LC record available at https://lccn.loc.gov/2021052391

ISBN: 978-0-367-63637-1 (hbk)
ISBN: 978-0-367-63642-5 (pbk)
ISBN: 978-1-003-12006-3 (ebk)

DOI: 10.4324/9781003120063

Typeset in Bembo
by KnowledgeWorks Global Ltd.

For Vincent and Livian, in the hope of a more democratic future for them and for all the children to come.

CONTENTS

Preface *viii*

1 Living and Learning in an Age of Global Crisis   1

2 Is This the End of the Democratic Dream?   30

3 Pandemics and Populism in a Post-Truth World   59

4 A Self-Made Climate Catastrophe   85

5 Propositions for Democratic Schooling   107

Index *129*

PREFACE

A book is a curious object. It is bound by its temporal, conceptual and linguistic arrangements, brought into being through the will of an author, and the days and weeks and months spent poring over every word in an attempt to fashion a coherent argument that might possibly resonate with others. Yet, a book is much more. It is a voyage of the mind, which does not always end at the intended destination, and possibly does not end at all. This is such a book, I think. What began as a proposal to the publisher in early 2020 to write a book that would build upon some scholarly work I had been engaged in around the possibilities of democratisation through schooling—which, by its institutional formulation in contemporary societies is anything but a democratic, public space of difference and affirmation for young people to become critical and creative agents of social change—has coalesced into something rather different to what was first intended.

I had many plans for 2020, including interstate research collaborations and international conferences, which rapidly unravelled thanks to the global pandemic. For example, I had programmed a second research summit that was planned for June 2020 called the 'Second Summit on Education for Democracy: Research, Policy, Practice & Activism', which was meant to build upon the 2017 'Re-imagining Education for Democracy Summit' and extend some of the lines of scholarly debate and inquiry that were generated from the initial event (e.g., Riddle, 2019; Riddle & Apple, 2019; Riddle & Heffernan, 2018). This book was supposed to be one of the outcomes that would arise from the second summit. Although the second summit had to be cancelled because of the pandemic, there have already been some generative outcomes from educators and scholar–activists who had planned to attend (e.g., Heggart & Kolber, 2022; Riddle et al., 2022), and hopefully, these produce further encounters of thought with educators, scholar–activists and others, in the spirit of working towards more democratic modes of living and learning together.

Over the course of 2020 and 2021, as we moved in and out of lockdown, I struggled with trying to entertain and educate two young children while working from home. Instead of focusing on my scholarly work, I spent much of 2020 doom scrolling my Twitter feed and watching daily televised press conferences with COVID case number updates, reading each new piece of worrying information about the epidemiological and public health issues unfolding, while becoming increasingly despondent about our federal government's gross mismanagement of quarantine and vaccine procurement. I attempted to make a start on the book multiple times during those first alarming months, but found myself unable to focus for more than a few minutes before returning to the eternal doom scroll of hot-takes by armchair epidemiologists and journalists.

However, by the end of 2020, when it became clear that the pandemic was not going away any time soon, I finally turned my mind to the task of writing this book. I began to draw together some of the threads that are developed and considered in the pages of this book. I found that as I got deeper into thinking and writing about schooling for democracy in a period of complex, interconnected global crises, it became more difficult to search for the places of hope and light, rather than staying in the grim, existential dread of calamitous climate change, ecological collapse, societal disintegration and rising authoritarian populism. My mood was dark for much of the period of writing this book. However, I have attempted to bring the book, and indeed my own thinking and affective state of being, back from the precipice over which one might surrender to the abyss. It has not been easy, and I think writing a book like this in the middle of a pandemic has exacerbated the tensions I experienced in trying to tackle in a scholarly work, what are grave, existential crises facing human societies this century, in the hope to open up thought to new horizons of possibility through democratic modes of schooling and living and working together with young people.

This book is my attempt to think through the following problem: Given the global rise of anti-democratic forces in the first decades of the twenty-first century, what should be the response of formal schooling to address these complex local–global crises? Contemporary liberal–democratic societies face a time of unprecedented political, economic and social challenges. Although there is a long tradition of scholarship regarding education and democracy—with its contemporary roots in the work of John Dewey, Michael Apple, Henry Giroux and others—the current global context requires a critical re-examination of the affordances, constraints, possibilities and contradictions of liberalist democratic values and the social institution of formal schooling. Societies are faced with multiple complex challenges at the start of the third decade of the twenty-first century, which demand a range of responses, including how formal schooling is framed as a public project to produce critical and engaged young people with the collective commitment to tackle the effects of the global climate crisis, growing social and economic inequality, political instability, insecurity, fear and hate.

This book attempts to consider the role of schooling as a public project to re-imagine democratic societies in more sustainable, collective and active ways to present a series of propositions for schooling that is for democracy. I believe that if there is hope to be found, such hope rests with children and young people. They are the ones who will need to rise to face the challenges of the twenty-first century. However, they have been persistently and consistently let down and lied to by those who remain in positions of power—the corporate oligarchs, elites and political class—who continue to engage in planetary and social exploitation and vandalism, all in the name of profit for a select few. The costs of taking action against the de-democratisation of society are high; the costs of doing nothing and accepting the hegemony of the neoliberal capitalist status quo are entirely unacceptable. As an educator, scholar and parent, I hope that this book provides others with a language that helps them to take up the local and global struggles to ensure that young people all over the world can become critical and creative agents of change, working together in collaborative and generatively democratic ways to tackle the complex set of crises facing them, so that they may not simply survive, but thrive over the coming years and decades.

References

Heggart, K., & Kolber, S. (Eds.). (2022). *Empowering teachers and democratising schooling*. Springer.

Riddle, S. (2019). Democracy and education in local–global contexts. *The International Education Journal: Comparative Perspectives, 18*(1), 1–6.

Riddle, S., & Apple, M. W. (Eds.). (2019). *Re-imagining education for democracy*. Routledge.

Riddle, S., & Heffernan, A. (2018). Education and democracy for complex contemporary childhoods. *Global Studies of Childhood, 8*(4), 319–324. https://doi.org/10.1177/2043610618817370

Riddle, S., Heffernan, A., & Bright, D. (Eds.). (2022). *New perspectives on education for democracy: Creative responses to local and global challenges*. Routledge.

1
LIVING AND LEARNING IN AN AGE OF GLOBAL CRISIS

Introduction

> One cannot foretell the surprises or disappointments the future has in store. … There may be tragic economic struggles, grim grapplings of race with race and class with class. It may be that 'private enterprise' will refuse to learn the lesson of service without some quite catastrophic revolution. … We do not know; we cannot tell. These are unnecessary disasters, but they may be unavoidable disasters. Human history becomes more and more, a race between education and catastrophe.
>
> *(Wells, 1922, p. 1100)*

During the final decade or so of the twentieth century—amid the crumbling Soviet Union and the fall of the Berlin Wall—it seemed a truism that 'history' had reached its end point (Fukuyama, 1989) and that the victory of liberal capitalist democracy over other forms of social, political and economic life was complete. Not only had communism been dealt a death blow in the collapse of the Soviet Union but the totalitarian horrors of fascism and Nazism were fast receding from immediate memory. This 'unabashed victory of economic and political liberalism' could be witnessed in 'the total exhaustion of viable systematic alternatives to Western liberalism' (Fukuyama, 1989, p. 3). It seemed evident that the globalising free market had brought economic prosperity to all corners of the world, and liberal democracy had become established as 'the only coherent political aspiration that spans different regions and cultures around the globe' (Fukuyama, 1992, p. xiv).

However, the triumph of the Western liberal–democratic dream has been short-lived, as the first two decades of the twenty-first century have clearly shown, through such events as the endless War on Terror™ and its devastating effects in Iraq, Syria, Afghanistan and elsewhere; the calamitous fallout from the 2008 US subprime mortgage bubble and the collapse of the financial industry, which precipitated the global financial crisis and spurred on the global Occupy movement; and more recently, the growing urgency of a climate catastrophe already underway and the inability or reluctance of liberal–democratic and capitalist institutions to respond in an effective and timely manner. In 2014, UN Secretary General Ban Ki-moon, in an address to the UN General Assembly, claimed that the world was 'living in an era of unprecedented level of crises' (Borger, 2014).

Over the past two decades, liberal democracies in places such as Australia, the UK and US have witnessed the erosion of democratic institutions and principles, while also facing yet failing to adequately respond to significant local and global challenges, including a global pandemic, ecological breakdown, rising economic inequality, social unrest and political instability. There is substantial evidence of the corrosion of democracy and liberalism in many societies as sociopolitical and socioeconomic foundations have been destabilised through multiple crises and conflicts during the first two decades of the twenty-first century. The current context is dangerous and uncertain, which makes it important to encourage more widespread democratic participation and action. Clearly, when it comes to the question of how societies should address the big issues facing them, 'business-as-usual is not going to be good enough. We need a radical reimagining of the role of the public in generating collective social good. Education generally, and schooling more specifically, must be a central part of such a project' (Riddle & Cleaver, 2017, p. 12).

Sardar (2010) claimed that we are now living in *postnormal* times, which are 'characterised by uncertainty, rapid change, realignment of power, upheaval and chaotic behaviour' (p. 435). The concept provides a useful perspective on how we might think through the accelerating pace of change and an increasing sense of crisis during the twenty-first century. These changes and crises are neither incremental nor isolated but simultaneous and interconnected (Sardar & Sweeney, 2016). The COVID-19 global pandemic provides a salient example of a postnormal phenomenon because it combines the features of postnormativity: Crisis, complexity, contradiction, alongside speed, scope, scale and simultaneity of rapidly accelerating change (Jones et al., 2021).

In the opening chapter to our book, *Re-imagining Education for Democracy*, Michael Apple and I argued:

> There is little doubt that we have reached a point in the global milieu where the multiple collapsing systems that upheld much of the previous century are beginning to be felt in profound ways. Capitalism, long lauded as the means for creating lasting economic prosperity and raising the working class up to a massified consumer class, has been rupturing through multiple financial collapses and the complete runaway corporate terrorism of the past decades. Liberalism, the ideological mainstay of Western democracies,

is rapidly being replaced by hyper-evangelical, neo-conservative and populist movements that are built on platforms of hate, segregation and fear of the Other. All over the world, there is a tilt to fascist, racist and misogynist forms of tyranny and oppression. This is to say nothing of the collapsing environmental ecosystems, on which our very existence depends. We are living in dangerous times.

(Riddle & Apple, 2019, p. 1)

This book extends on the opening move described above to consider how education, and in particular the formalised institutions of schooling for young people, might respond to the complexities of the twenty-first century and its immediate and longer-term challenges. The main thesis prosecuted in this book is that schooling *for* democracy offers potential opportunities to meaningfully connect young people's learning to their lives in ways that go beyond the notion of formal schooling functioning simply as a provider of a future workforce and compliant citizenry.

This book takes as its starting point the challenge of education—with a focus on schooling—being for democracy in a time of collapsing societal and environmental systems. It considers the possible response of education to the multiple crises facing society and the planet through the radical re-democratisation of schooling. Schools have long been studied as potential sites of democracy, with mixed success. The current context demands a more radical set of democratic principles and practices, which can be nurtured within schools and other formal and informal sites of education. This book also addresses the tensions and potential contradictions in schools, which can easily operate as social sites of exclusion and 'citizenship building', which reproduce existing social inequalities, while standardising and reducing the capacity for young people to express themselves in diverse, democratic ways. Additionally, this book considers the ways in which young people can engage in direct action, civil disobedience and resistance, which offer hope and the potential of collective democratic action through movements such as the Extinction Rebellion civil disobedience activities (Extinction Rebellion, 2019) and School Strike for Climate protests (Boulianne et al., 2020).

This book combines radical democratic theories to develop an innovative and contemporary conceptual framework with which to address the problem of a schooling that is for democracy, pointing to the possibilities, limits and tensions of attempting to reimagine education in more inclusive, collective and sustainable ways through democratic action. This book explores and examines how more critically democratic educational policies and practices and the daily activities of learners, educators, leaders, communities and societies can work towards collective well-being, increased civic participation and a common commitment to an ecologically sustainable engagement with the planet. This book also shares accounts of the struggles and engagements of young people, which demonstrate productive new expressions of hopeful encounters in local and global communities and produce a plurality of possibilities regarding more democratic ways of living and learning together.

This book presents one possible response to the question: Given the global rise of anti-democratic forces in the first decades of the twenty-first century, what should be the response of schooling to address these complex local–global crises? We face a time of unprecedented political, economic and social challenges. As such, this book considers the role of schooling as a public project to reimagine democratic societies in more sustainable, collective and active ways. Through a mixture of theoretical, conceptual and empirical analyses, this book presents a series of propositions for schooling that is for democracy.

However, this is not a book that makes a case for a democratic utopia as some kind of a simple answer to a complex set of problems. To do so would be to do a grave disservice to democracy, with all of its contradictions and tensions. One is reminded of Ursula LeGuin's (1975) warning of the hidden cost behind the lure of simple utopian thought in *The Ones Who Walk Away from Omelas*, a cautionary tale about the terrible price paid for the citizens of Omelas to live in a state of peace and joy, and those who choose to renounce such a bargain. As described in the short story, it is true that the citizens of Omelas possessed:

> A boundless and generous contentment, a magnanimous triumph felt not against some outer enemy but in communion with the finest and fairest in the souls of all men everywhere and the splendor of the world's summer: this is what swells the hearts of the people of Omelas, and the victory they celebrate is that of life.
>
> *(LeGuin, 1975, p. 255)*

However, for the great many citizens of Omelas to live in such utopian bliss required the misery and suffering of the few. This is both a perversion of equality and democracy, and one which has resonances in the structural flaws of contemporary political, economic and social structures to be found in liberal–democratic societies. We can, and must, do better. We can, and must, find new ways of meaningfully engaging in the collective struggles of society to be more inclusive, equitable and just.

This book proceeds from the notion that we live in a time of multiple and interconnected crises, which are both globalised and localised in their causes, effects and potential solutions. Of course, saying that we live in a time of crisis is nothing new. For example, almost a century ago, Counts (1932) argued that 'we live in troublous times; we live in an age of profound change; we live in an age of revolution. Indeed it is highly doubtful whether man ever lived in a more eventful period than the present' (p. 31). However, when Counts wrote about whether the school dare to build a new social order roughly 90 years ago, the hydrogen bomb had not yet been invented, humans had not yet travelled to space, climate change was underway but not yet realised and the smartphone, microprocessor and Internet were matters for science fiction, not fact. Fast-forward to 2020, when during the thick of a global pandemic:

> We live at a time of multiple plagues that fuel the current coronavirus epidemic that is engulfing the globe inflicting economic misery, suffering and death as they move through societies with the speed of a deadly tornado. These include the plague of ecological destruction, the degradation of civic culture, the possibility of a nuclear war, and the normalization of a brutal culture of cruelty. Moreover, the plague of neoliberalism has waged a full-scale attack on the welfare state. In doing so, it has underfunded and weakened those institutions such as education and the public health sector. In addition, it has removed the vast majority of [people] from the power relations and modes of governance that would enable them to deal critically and intelligently with natural disasters, pandemics, and a slew of planetary crises which cannot be addressed by the market. In the midst of this pandemic, the poison of ruling-class power is at the center of the current political, ideological, and medical crisis.
>
> *(Giroux, 2020, np)*

Taking his argument further, Giroux (2020) claimed that our contemporary age of crisis is driven by a pedagogy of moral indifference and the collapse of civic culture. He contended that 'we are in the midst of not simply a political crisis, but also an educational crisis in which matters of power, governance, knowledge and a disdain for truth and evidence have wreaked havoc' (Giroux, 2020, np). The continued rise and rise of alt-right, White supremacist and neofascist groups in places such as the US, South America, Europe and Australia sit alongside widely shared, hyperventilating posts on social media from anti-vaccination campaigners and conspiracy theorists, which are fuelled by irrational fear and hate, alongside a logic of single-minded social destruction, yet find a compliant and willing audience online. It seems imperative that such a state of affairs, combined with 'the rise of neo-fascism and increasing global tensions require us to consider how we might better inoculate societies from the social diseases of war, inequality, and potential social collapse' (Riddle & Apple, 2019, p. 1).

In a 2015 address to the *Cities for Tomorrow Conference*, the Rockefeller Foundation president Judith Rodin argued that 'there are three global forces colliding to make crisis the new normal': Rapid urbanisation, globalisation and climate change. Rodin (2015) went on to claim that 'we are more connected than ever before. Contagions—health, financial, or otherwise—don't respect borders' (np). Given the disruptive global effects of the COVID-19 pandemic during 2020 and 2021, these comments appear particularly prescient. It seems that perhaps more than ever, as Wells (1922) cautioned, we truly are in a race between education and catastrophe. At this stage, it is unclear whether education or catastrophe will prevail.

On Crisis

The etymology of the word 'crisis' provides useful definitional grounding for the propositions that are made in this book. Originating from the Greek κρίσις (*krísis*), meaning 'decision', the word was Latinised to *crisis*, which refers to the turning point in a disease, at which a person either recovers or dies from their illness. Contemporary usage of the concept is widespread and varied, although 'crisis' commonly refers to a moment at which difficult or dangerous change occurs and some kind of choice must be made or a decision is required. Crisis can also express the end of an epoch and the moment of immanent transition, with 'various temporal beginnings and whose unknown future seems to give free scope to all sorts of wishes and anxieties, fears and hope. "Crisis" becomes a structural signature of modernity' (Koselleck & Richter, 2006, p. 372). Further, Gardels and Berggruen (2019) claimed that history has reached an inflection point, in which 'we live either on the cusp of an entirely new era or on the brink of a return to an all-too-familiar, regressive, and darker past. How to reconcile these opposite trends is the daunting summons for governance in the decades ahead' (p. 9).

Similarly, Gramsci (1971) argued that 'crisis consists precisely in the fact that the old is dying and the new cannot be born; in this interregnum a great variety of morbid symptoms appear' (pp. 275–276). It is perhaps too early to say how long the present interregnum will last, and certainly nobody knows for certain what the 'new' will look like when we reach the other side. All that we can say with confidence is that we are living in a time of great morbidity. There is both destructive and productive potential in the concept of crisis, which is why it provides an important conceptual overlay for the argument presented in this book—that schooling for democracy lies at the heart of the project for a more sustainable and engaged commitment to the future.

Arendt (1969) argued for the productive nature of crisis, in which it 'requires from us either new or old answers, but in any case direct judgments. A crisis becomes a disaster only when we respond to it with preformed judgments, that is, with prejudices' (p. 174). Importantly, crisis requires both the perception of the crisis by actors—such as people, institutions or states—and the specific mediation and performance of those actors in response to crisis (Moffitt, 2015). Clearly, 'crises have material bases, but it is their perception, interpretation and discursive construction by actors that make an event recognisable as a crisis. All crises are lived experiences, mediated through language and cognition' (Voltolini et al., 2020, p. 615). It is in this agentic responsiveness and lived experience that we might find a way through the contemporary complex set of crises, and the task for this book is to investigate the role of the school and its potential for democratic becoming.

In addition, Lipscy (2020) claimed that crises compel people to make important decisions under pressure, including temporal pressure and the threat of unknown social, political and economic consequences. He also contended that crises were on the increase, and that international crisis contagion was a new fixture of economic globalisation and the rapid transfer of communication, knowledge, people and goods around the world, which means that a localised crisis can rapidly become a globalised crisis. Two pertinent examples are the 2008 global financial crisis and the 2020–2022 COVID-19 pandemic. Clearly, we have come to a very dangerous moment in history, in which multiple interconnected crises have arrived and now demand answers from us. It remains to be seen how we do so.

On Democracy, (Neo)Liberalism and Capitalism

Fukuyama's (1989) oft-quoted claim that history had reached its end point with the triumph of capitalism over communism now appears to be not simply premature but to have entirely misread the political and economic undercurrents of the time. The argument that liberal democracy had emerged as the sole legitimate form of political, economic and social governance had obvious appeal to the political class and corporate oligarchists because it enabled them to engage in an unchecked concentration of wealth and power through globalised corporate hegemony during the final two decades of the twentieth century and most of the first decade of the twenty-first century. That is, until the global financial crisis laid bare the lie of endless growth, casino capitalism (Giroux, 2010b) and predatory corporate hegemony and massive fictitious wealth (Bresser-Pereira, 2010). However, not all were taken with the triumphalism of the late-twentieth century. For example, Mouffe (1993) cautioned:

> Not long ago we were being told, to the accompaniment of much fanfare, that liberal democracy had won and that history had ended. Alas, far from having produced a smooth transition to pluralist democracy, the collapse of communism seems, in many places, to have opened the way to a resurgence of nationalism and the emergence of new antagonisms. Western democrats view with astonishment the explosion of manifold ethnic, religious and nationalist conflicts that they thought belonged to a bygone age. Instead of the heralded 'New World Order', the victory of universal values, and the generalization of 'post-conventional' identities, we are witnessing an explosion of particularisms and an increasing challenge to Western universalism.
>
> *(p. 1)*

Similarly, Chomsky (2003) argued against the prevailing logic of the globalised free market and liberal democracy as the hegemonic doctrine, to say that 'the reality is that the world, including our own society, is moving toward a more autocratic and absolutist structure. The scope of the public arena is narrowing [and] democracy is under attack' (p. 236). The implicit consensus of the value of democracy is under great threat from multiple forces (Doorenspleet, 2019), which raises the question of why there is a shift towards more repressive, authoritarian and populist forms of political governance at a time when democratic ideals are widely touted as being the only legitimate form.

To consider first why democracy is in a state of crisis and second, how schooling might be for democracy, it is necessary to generate some initial propositions about the concept of democracy and its construction within contemporary political and social discourses. Similarly, concepts of (neo)liberalism and capitalism deserve consideration and critique to determine their present formations and the ways in which they have come to be so. This section begins the discussion about democracy, liberalism and capitalism, which is extended in Chapter 2's analyses of the crisis of the Western democratic dream. This is done to provide context for the propositions regarding how schooling can be for democracy and its potential as a site of progressive reform and social change.

It is difficult to arrive at a suitable definition of democracy that does not fall into the trap of taking contemporary political, social and economic formations labelled as 'democracy' as being a given and inherent good. Indeed, the concept of democracy is contested and could be described as a sliding signifier, by which it is given and gives meaning, dependent on the context and intent of its usage. Perhaps Nancy (2011) put it best:

> *Democracy* has become an exemplary case of the loss of the power to signify: representing both supreme political virtue and the only means of achieving the common good, it grew so fraught that it was no longer capable of generating any problematic or serving any heuristic purpose. All that goes on now is marginal debate about the differences between various democratic systems and sensibilities. In short, *democracy* means everything—politics, ethics, law, civilization—and nothing.
>
> (p. 58)

In a theoretical review of over 300 papers on education and democracy, Sant (2019) identified eight different typologies of democratic education: Elitist, liberal, neoliberal, deliberative, multiculturalist, participatory, critic and agonistic. Brown (2011) argued that democracy is an unfinished principle, which has become an empty signifier, too open and vacuous in practice and meaning, and that capitalism 'has finally reduced democracy to a brand, a late modern twist on commodity fetishism' (p. 44). Similarly, Amsler (2015) claimed that democracy is ontologically unstable and constantly changing, while a more radical democracy enables the fluidity and contestation to be foregrounded and embraced. Further, Apple (2018) argued that there are competing forms of 'thin' and 'thick' democracy:

> 'Thick' understandings of democracy that seek to provide full collective participation in the search for the common good and the creation of critical citizens are up against 'thin', market-oriented versions of consumer

choice, possessive individualism, and an education that is valued largely as a tool for meeting a set of limited economic needs as defined by the powerful.

(pp. 4–5)

While there is no clear and easy definition of the concept of democracy, for the purposes of the arguments presented in this book, a particular construction of the concept is developed below. The lineage for this construction of democracy is intimately tied to its relationship to education and engages with the thought of scholars such as Dewey (1899, 1916), Mouffe (1993, 2019), Freire (1972), Apple (2006, 2011, 2013, 2018), Agamben (2011), Giroux (2009, 2010a, 2010b, 2016, 2020) and Rancière (2006, 2010). Democracy necessarily requires an ontological position of plurality and productive dissent as the grounding framework of a democratic politics, in which civic responsibility and collective action are grounded within the historical, cultural and social realities of communities. It also takes the starting point that contemporary liberal democracy 'results from the coupling of two heterogeneous elements, a politico–juridical rationality and an economic–governmental rationality' (Agamben, 2011, p. 4), which forms both the broader constitution of the body politic and institutions of social governance, rather than simply the form of state politics.

Sant (2019) argued for the moral and instrumental appeal of liberal democracy in its merger of individual liberty, equality and popular sovereignty. Similarly, Ferrara (2014) claimed that the potential of democracy lies in its capacity for openness and transformation, through which innovation is valued over tradition. In their work on democratic education, Beane and Apple (2007) argued that 'democracy is not something out there waiting to be reached. Rather it is in the work itself as we create ways to promote human dignity, equity, justice, and critical action' (p. 25). Democracy exists within the context of communities and groups of people participating in collective action for the public good and to form a commons. It does not exist as some external force or institutionalised system of power and dominance, although such systems are often mislabelled as being democratic. Beane and Apple's (2007) work drew upon and made explicit the practical realities of teachers and students living the democratic ideals arising from seminal theorising of democracy and education that was conducted nearly a century ago:

> A democracy is more than a form of government; it is primarily a mode of associated living, of conjoint communicated experience. The extension in space of the number of individuals who participate in an interest so that each has to refer his own action to that of others, and to consider the action of others to give point and direction to his own, is equivalent to the breaking down of those barriers of class, race, and national territory which kept men from perceiving the full import of their activity.
>
> *(Dewey, 1916, p. 101)*

Rancière has engaged in the theoretical and philosophical question of democracy across much of his work, arguing that much of what we call democracy in contemporary societies is little more than massified individualism, in which consumer culture replaces democratic participation, and the right to make choices between almost identical products in a marketplace is replicated across politics, economics and other social encounters. Instead, what we refer to as a democratic government 'may be called democracy but it is in actual fact an aristocracy' (Rancière, 2010, p. 45). Further, Rancière (2010) argued that 'democracy is not a political regime … democracy is the very institution of politics itself—of its subject and of the form of its relationship' (p. 32). Rancière (2006) explained:

> The term democracy, then, does not strictly designate either a form of society or a form of government. 'Democratic society' is never anything but an imaginary portrayal designed to support this or that principle of good government. Societies, today as yesterday, are organized by the play of oligarchies. There is, strictly speaking, no such thing as democratic government. Government is always exercised by the minority over the majority. The 'power of the people' is therefore necessarily also heterotopic to inegalitarian society and to oligarchic government. It is what divides government from itself by dividing society from itself. It is therefore also what separates the exercise of government from the representation of society.
>
> *(Rancière, 2006, p. 52)*

Agamben (2011) contended that democracy serves a two-fold purpose: Being the form of legitimation of power and the manner in which power is democratically exercised. Both the body politic and the functions of governance can be, but are not necessarily, democratic. However, what is generally referred to as democracy is the process of electing state representative legislatures and executives to various forms of 'democratic' parliaments around the globe. Yet, this dual understanding of democracy as both a form of government and a form of body politic is fraught and often contradictory. For example, take Rancière's (2010) claim, that 'the contemporary way of stating the "democratic paradox" is thus: democracy as a form of government is threatened by democracy as a form of social and political life and so the former must repress the latter' (p. 47). The power of the body politic must be held at bay by the institutions, traditions and practices of the powerful elite who are 'elected' to govern for the people. Importantly, Rancière's (2006) analysis in *Hatred of Democracy* exposed the fantasy at the heart of the modern liberal capitalist democratic dream, in which he argued:

> We are accustomed to hearing that democracy is the worst of governments with the exception of all the others. But the new antidemocratic sentiment gives the general formula a more troubling expression. Democratic government, it says, is bad when it is all owed to be corrupted by democratic society, which wants for everyone to be equal and for all differences to be

respected. It is good, on the other hand, when it rallies individuals enfeebled by democratic society to the vitality of war in order to defend the values of civilization, the values pertaining to the clash of civilizations. The thesis of the new hatred of democracy can be succinctly put: there is only one good democracy, the one that represses the catastrophe of democratic civilization.

(p. 4)

The anti-democratic sentiment is perhaps most apparent in the rise of protofascist tendencies in many places around the globe, and even more blatant neofascist political parties gaining footholds in parliaments. Far-right populism is entwined with anti-immigration rhetoric, White supremacy ideology, racism and misogyny, which combine to form a toxic mixture. Mouffe (2019) argued that traditional social–democratic parties have been unable to grasp the nature of the threat posed by populism and have instead remained caught in the failed policies of neoliberalism. She continued:

> It is in the post-democratic context of the erosion of the democratic ideals of popular sovereignty and equality that the 'populist movement' should be apprehended. It is characterized by the emergence of manifold resistances against a politico–economic system that is increasingly perceived as being controlled by privileged elites who are deaf to the demands of the other groups in society.
>
> *(Mouffe, 2019, p. 18)*

Neoliberalism is also important to consider, in terms of its formation as a politics of liberal democracy that is entirely articulated through the logics of financial capitalism (Mouffe, 2019), in which everything, including education, becomes a market (Connell, 2013) and is subject to the tenets of free-market enterprise. Carr and Thésée (2019) contended that neoliberalised social democracy has become a normative, hegemonic democracy, which considers education as a function of preparing future workers for the job market rather than an expression of social justice and the struggle to address social inequities. They wondered whether the contemporary moment enables the thinking of viable alternatives to normative, hegemonic democracy.

Further, Giroux (2020) argued that neoliberalism's 'virulent ideology of extreme competitiveness and irrational selfishness, and its impatience with matters of ethics, justice and truth has undermined critical thought and the power of informed judgment' (np). Instead, within a neoliberal formation of market-based ideology, democracy becomes a commodity to be bought and sold, advertised and marketed to the consumer–voter, who then makes a choice between relatively similar choices in the political market—much like the choice between purchasing a red sedan or a blue sedan from a car dealership. Rancière (2006) described this as being the apolitical life of the commodified society, which renders the body politic into a homogenous mass, while the atomisation of individuals renders them separate and yet, wholly integrated into the mass. Within this mass, the political and social become indistinguishable from the massified individuals who reside within a contemporary society (Rancière, 2010), distracted and docile, kept to strict functions as units of production and consumption, rather than critical and creative citizens within a vibrant polity.

Amsler (2015) presented a compelling case for capitalism and neoliberalism as technologies of harm, which make people, animals, ecosystems and the entire environment sick. In stark contrast, Apple (2006) has argued for the importance of public institutions as being central to caring, democratic societies, in which markets and market relations are subordinate to the public good and the production of a thick democracy. Further, neoliberal rationalities of capitalist governance pervert social justice to its own ends, namely that of increasing the concentration of wealth and power in the hands of the corporate oligarchs, supported by systems of political donation, influence and a revolving door of political staffers, lobbyists, media and politicians. The edifice is built on a lie of meritocracy, which sits in contrast to the principles of equality and democracy (Arendt, 1969), and which favours certain individuals—namely White men born and raised in elite socioeconomic contexts—while excluding others, such as women, people of colour, Indigenous peoples, poor people and those who are considered surplus to society (Bauman, 2017). Further, those who are considered to be surplus are also considered to be disposable:

> Such populations are often warehoused in schools that resemble boot camps, dispersed to dank and dangerous workplaces far from the enclaves of the tourist industries, incarcerated in prisons that privilege punishment over rehabilitation, and consigned to the status of the permanently unemployed. Rendered redundant as a result of the collapse of the social state, a pervasive racism, a growing disparity in income and wealth, and a take-no-prisoners neoliberalism, an increasing number of individuals and groups are being demonized, criminalized, or simply abandoned, either by virtue of their status as immigrants or because they are young, poor, unemployed, disabled, homeless, or stuck in low-paying jobs.
>
> *(Giroux, 2009, p. 9)*

Social and economic inequalities are essential features of neoliberal–capitalist societies, in spite of the fundamental tension with democratic equality. Dorling (2019) prosecuted the argument that income inequality is the greatest social threat of contemporary times, and importantly, that it is a deliberate *choice* of societies to allow gross inequality to persist. The richest one per cent utilise the vast resources available to them to support their heartfelt support for the argument that greed is justifiable, and that if everyone simply worked harder and smarter, they too could get ahead. The clichéd 'American Dream' is a perfect example of how ingrained this myth has become.

Yet, all is not well. Social and economic inequalities are rising, and along with the physical and cultural displacement of large groups of people, the notion of a surplus population (Bauman, 2017) is becoming entrenched in the politics of many nation states. The working class has become the working poor and the unemployed continue to be the undeserving poor, living below the poverty line in wealthy countries like Australia and the US. Dorling (2015) argued that persistent social inequality is built into the ideological fabric of contemporary society, in which injustice is defended as being a necessary effect of the meritocratic and competitive forces of neoliberalism and capitalism. The mantra of 'greed is good' works just fine for the elite but wreaks havoc on those who have neither the economic nor cultural resources to take personal advantage of structural inequality.

The COVID-19 pandemic has exacerbated almost every facet of social and economic inequalities—along lines of nationality, race, class and gender—laying bare the greed that sits at the heart of the capitalist project. Coy (2021) argued that a long-term result of COVID-19 exacerbating already existing inequality is that 'the least advantaged will suffer the most in damaged health, derailed schooling, and wrecked careers' (np). At the same time, the super-rich have profited enormously from the pandemic. As one example of many, the collective worth of billionaires in the US rose 44 per cent from the start of the pandemic in March 2020 to March 2021, increasing from US $2.9 trillion to $4.2 trillion in a single year (Collins, 2021).

To say that the gap between the rich and poor has widened is an understatement. Indeed, the rapid worsening of inequality during the pandemic prompted the International Monetary Fund to warn that if governments do not take steps to ameliorate some of the worst effects of social and economic inequalities, 'societies may experience rising polarisation, erosion of trust in government, or social unrest' (Inman, 2021, np). Further, Dorling (2015) argued that inequality is sustained by elitism, exclusion, prejudice, greed and despair. It is a matter of choice, rather than a given, that widespread social and economic inequalities continue to define contemporary liberal–democratic societies. Indeed, McLaren and Farahmandpur (2005) made the argument that neoliberal policymaking has been responsible for further widening inequality:

> Neoliberal reformers and regional integrationists have launched a front, no-holds-barred attack on social justice, accelerating the incapacity of individuals to recognize capital's internal logic of accumulation and diminishing the power of individuals to counter the pressure of vested corporate interests and the politics of the capitalist class while at the same time mystifying the entire process by linking democracy to the so-called natural pulsations of the market.
>
> *(p. 38)*

As inequality continues to rise, so does fear, mistrust and apathy in governments and social institutions, including schools and other formal and informal sites of education. Support for democracy also decreases as societies become more unequal. Dorling (2015) made the prescient point that fears of things such as worldwide recession, pandemics, war and other large-scale suffering increase with growing inequality, which further increases mistrust of others and a lack of confidence in governments and other public institutions. Additionally, as greed and inequality have become entrenched in the ideological apparatus of contemporary neoliberal–capitalist democracies, so too has a malaise of despair at the seemingly intractable elitism, prejudice and exclusion (Dorling, 2015).

Mounk (2018) argued that there has long been an exhausted disillusionment with politics, which has been taken as a baseline affective register of the electorate. However, there is now a sense of growing disdain, restlessness and anger, from which the growth of populist and authoritarian movements find increasing support as voters turn away from liberal democracy in search of something else (Mounk, 2018). Concurring, Monbiot (2018) claimed that:

> If politics as usual no longer delivers, people look elsewhere for answers. This 'elsewhere' often means demagoguery: movements characterised by the extreme simplification of political choices, the abandonment of reasoned argument, and scapegoating. The reaction against democratic failure has licensed a clutch of suppressed hatreds—of women, immigrants, racial and religious minorities, difference of all kinds. We witness the resurgence of the kind of politics that until recently seemed to be everywhere in retreat.
> *(p. 22)*

It seems clear that the triumph of twentieth-century capitalism and liberal democracy was a short-lived victory, if it ever was truly a victory at all. However, this raises the question of what is to come next. The rise of protofascist movements across the globe, alongside increasing ignorance, fear and resentment, growing racism, xenophobia and misogyny—expressed clearly in widespread growing support for religious extremism, White supremacy, populism and demagoguery—demonstrates that something is clearly amiss. We cannot afford to act as if everything will be alright because we live in supposedly free, liberal and democratic societies. We cannot leave things to continue as they are and hope for the best because the crises facing all peoples are too large to ignore. We must act now to avoid catastrophe. Therefore, this book focuses on how young people hold the promise of a more sustainable and democratic future. Education broadly and formal schooling specifically are central to how we choose to prepare young people for a world of complex challenges and multiple crises over the coming decades.

On Young People and Education

> What the best and wisest parent wants for his own child, that must the community want for all of its children. Any other ideal for our schools is narrow and unlovely; acted upon, it destroys our democracy. All that

society has accomplished for itself is put, through the agency of the school, at the disposal of its future members. All its better thoughts of itself it hopes to realize through the new possibilities thus opened to its future self. Here individualism and socialism are at one.

(Dewey, 1899, p. 19)

Contemporary childhood and adolescence is a time of great change, struggle and becoming for young people, which is 'simultaneously filled with possibilities and fraught with dangerous tensions as the big social apparatuses that drove much of the last century—Capitalism, Liberalism, Democracy—seem to be struggling, and in some places, entirely coming apart' (Riddle & Heffernan, 2018, p. 319). Young people face enormous uncertainty and instability, with the challenges of the twenty-first century weighing heavily on their futures. The children coming into classrooms today will be those who will need the skills and knowledge to tackle the great challenges and existential threats of catastrophic climate change and ecological collapse, growing social and economic inequalities and dangerous political instability. Therefore, it is imperative that education in all its forms, and schooling especially, rises to the challenge of helping young people to face these challenges. Society owes it to young people to provide them with the wherewithal to understand and tackle the complex crises that will define this century.

However, Giroux (2009) argued that the prevailing neoliberal social order has replaced social responsibility and compassion with fear and punishment as the driving forces of the relationship of young people to society. A market-oriented view of young people considers them as little more than consumers to be marketed to or as a source of cheap future labour. The notion of education as being an important social investment in the futures of young people is replaced by the desire for 'job-ready graduates' and the commodification of young people themselves, which is driven by a philosophy of money rather than a commitment to justice and civic responsibility, 'in which everything, including the worth of young people, is measured through the potentially barbaric calculations of finance, exchange value, and profitability' (Giroux, 2009, p. 42). The hopes and dreams of young people are boxed up, commodified and then marketed and sold back to young people in the name of profit and corporate avarice.

For children and adolescents living in poverty, and for Black, Indigenous and other racialised and minoritised young people, the situation is dire. Youth incarceration rates are at shocking levels in wealthy countries such as the US and Australia, which is an indictment on society. For example, Aboriginal and/or Torres Strait Islander youth in Australia represent six per cent of the population aged 10–17, yet account for 48 per cent of incarcerated young people, and are 17 times more likely to be in detention than non-Indigenous Australian youth (Australian Institute of Health and Welfare, 2021). The statistics are similarly shocking for Black youth in the US. Giroux (2009) was scathing in his analyses of how young people in the US, especially Latinx and Black youth, have been cast as *disposable* and treated as necessary by-products of the neoliberal–capitalist system. The treatment of young Indigenous and Black youth as disposable and marginalised others is at odds with the egalitarian promise at the heart of democracy and espoused by 'free' Western societies such as the US and Australia.

I have previously argued that 'education is at the heart of our efforts to reconfigure the social apparatus in more equitable and socially just ways, for both the sustainability of our communities and the planet' (Riddle, 2019, p. 3). This book is premised on the belief that education, and schooling in particular, should be at the centre of a reconfiguration of society to address the multiple crises besetting the planet and humanity. Education is a powerful social and cultural force, which Connell (2012) has referred to as being dangerous because it shapes the future of society and the formation of culture in addition to its role in social and cultural reproduction. Education is not simply a force for indoctrinating young people into the social order but can also enable the creation of a new social order (Counts, 1932). Further, 'education is a political act, even education that seeks to be bland, neutral and nonpartisan' (Smith, 1995, p. 66). The acts of teaching and learning are thoroughly radical acts of belief and commitment to the promise of the future, so there is much possibility for greater democratic becoming through education as a site of social change.

Giroux (2010a) argued that education is never neutral, nor should it be. Instead, education 'is always directive in its attempt to teach students to inhabit a particular mode of agency, enable them to understand the larger world and one's role in it in a specific way, define their relationship, if not responsibility, to diverse others, and experience in the classroom some sort of understanding of a more just, imaginative, and democratic life' (Giroux, 2010a, p. 718). At the same time, it is important to not assume that education is an 'unfailing remedy for every ill to which man is subject, whether it be vice, crime, war, poverty, riches, injustice, racketeering, political corruption, race hatred, class conflict, or just plain original sin' (Counts, 1932, p. 3). While schooling can absolutely play a key role in the reconstruction of society, it cannot address all societal ills and does not stand alone as an inoculative mechanism to prevent social and economic inequalities, war and famine, political injustice or the devastating effects of climate change. However, schooling can and should be a central part of society's plan for a future built on sustainable collaboration between all people to ensure that the planet and society's future is assured. Schooling must be a compact between society and its young people, that the future can be shaped in more sustainable and inclusive ways through a commitment to democracy.

It is commonly argued that contemporary education systems serve two main functions: To prepare young people for the world of work and to equip them with the skills, knowledge and critical facilities to fully engage in society. However, there is often substantial differences between what schools are *expected* to do, what they *actually* do and perhaps what they *should* do (McMannon, 1997). Biesta (2015) claimed that 'the point of education is that students learn *something*, that they learn it for a *reason*, and that they learn it *from someone*' (p. 76), which raises questions regarding what young people are learning, from whom and for what reasons and purposes. The answers, of course, depend on who is asking the questions and which answers they seek when they ask such questions. Further, Arblaster (1972) suggested that there are three approaches to education—sustaining class structures, training for job-readiness and economic investment—in which education serves a function of 'sustaining and reinforcing the existing social and economic order' (p. 36). In contrast, Goodlad (1997) argued:

> *Education* is an adventure of the self. It is natural, then, to think of education as a matter of private purpose and experience. However, adventures of the self are experienced in public contexts. The self is shaped through interpretation of social encounters; the nature of these encounters is critically important. The private purposes of education—the cultivation and satisfaction of the self—can be pursued only in the company of public purpose. How we are with others has a great deal to do with how we are with ourselves.
>
> *(p. 155)*

Angus (1986) claimed that 'education was generally regarded as a means to promote democracy, social harmony, social mobility and equality' (p. 9) in Australian education policymaking and practice by the 1950s. Further, Carr and Hartnett (1996) argued that the primary purpose of education is to be a site of political reproduction, in which young people are educated to be free and equal citizens, understanding the principles of democracy and egalitarianism, so that they may collectively participate in the common good of society. While this sentiment resonates with contemporary civics and citizenship education theories, the issue of course is that society is neither egalitarian nor democratic. Additionally, there is little social harmony or social mobility on offer for those who are least advantaged by the present political, economic and social order.

Connell (1993) claimed that education is a key factor in the production of social hierarchies and the legitimation of inequality, which is premised on the notion of meritocracy within a neoliberal version of capitalism. The legitimation of inequality begins early and permeates everything within society's structures and institutions, including schooling. Two decades later, Connell (2013) argued:

> Neoliberalism has a definite view of education, understanding it as human capital formation. It is the business of forming the skills and attitudes needed by a productive workforce—productive in the precise sense of producing an ever-growing mass of profits for the market economy. 'Human capital' is a metaphor, and in itself too narrow. But this economistic idea does catch an important feature of education, that it is a creative process oriented to the future.
>
> *(p. 104)*

Arblaster (1972) claimed that while there is common acceptance of the principle of education being to 'imprint certain ideas and values upon the impressionable minds and characters of the young', there is cause for concern because 'once that principle is accepted, it is very difficult effectively to oppose those who are determined that education shall be a prop for the existing social and economic order, and who have the power and the money to ensure that it is so' (p. 39). There is power in curriculum in terms of how the knowledge base of young people is developed, and those who hold the keys to power have substantial influence over what gets taught in school, by whom and to whom, which has significant implications for the kinds of futures that can be imagined by and for young people. A counter-hegemonic curriculum is essential if schooling is to be reimagined in ways that better support all young people to become critical and creative citizens within a compassionate and caring community.

One concerning trend over the past few decades has been the increasing power over curriculum by a loose alliance of neoconservative, neoliberal and right-wing fundamentalist Christian forces. This phenomenon has been thoroughly documented in the context of the US in the work of Apple (2006, 2011, 2013, 2018), and has become increasingly apparent in the Australian context (e.g., Connell, 2013; McGregor, 2009; Taylor, 2013). The influence of *conservative modernisation*—'the complicated alliance behind the wave after wave of educational reforms that have centred around neo-liberal commitments to the market and a supposedly weak state, neo-conservative emphases on stronger control over curricula and values and "new managerial" proposals to install rigorous and reductive forms of accountability in schooling at all levels' (Apple, 2011, p. 22)—on education policymaking can be observed through effects such as narrowed curriculum, increased high-stakes standardised testing, school performance league tables and a discursive shift from teaching quality to teacher quality (Connell, 2012; Mockler, 2014). School vouchers and charter schools, alongside increased funnelling of public money into private schools, have further exacerbated the growing educational inequality (Bonnor & Shepherd, 2016).

Progressive and critical education scholars and activists have long viewed the school as a site of discursive and material struggle for the future of society and an opportunity to engage young people in meaningful democratic encounters. However, at the same time, the forces of neoliberalism, neoconservatism, Christian evangelism, authoritarian populism and market fundamentalism have combined to create a situation in which the marginalisation and disenfranchisement of young people perpetuates a system of gross injustice and growing inequality. Simultaneously, schools are expected to somehow address many of society's ills (Aronowitz, 2008). Education has existed in a state of near-constant crisis, although 'a crisis in education would at any time give rise to serious concern even if it did not reflect, as in the present instance it does, a more general crisis and instability in modern society' (Arendt, 1969, p. 185). Although Arendt wrote those words over 50 years ago, perhaps they are even more fitting now, when we face a time of unrelenting and extraordinary change, destabilisation and disruption.

Aronowitz and Giroux (1987) described a growing crisis in public education, which has eroded opportunities for young people to engage in critical and conceptual thinking as a necessary basis for democratic encounter. Their analyses demonstrate that the problem of education for democracy is neither recent nor easy to address. Despite the 1980s being considered by many to be the peak of Western liberalist, capitalist and democratic success, the cracks had already begun to show. The broader crisis 'has given rise to cynicism about the promise of democracy, to a vast and unequal distribution of ideological and material resources both in the schools and in the wider society' (Aronowitz & Giroux, 1991, p. 48), which has only increased since that time.

This brings us to the question of an education that is for democracy, and the role of schooling in providing young people with the knowledge and skills needed to address the complex crises facing them. There is an urgent need to reconfigure the social, economic and political apparatus of society, of which schooling is but one part. The destructive myth of endless growth that fuels predatory global capitalism, along with its calamitous effects on biodiversity, ecosystems and the climate, must be debunked as a matter of urgency. Additionally, economic systems that support and enable gross individual wealth accumulation and rampant greed must be replaced with economic systems that foster sustainability and reinvestment into the livelihoods of people within their local communities. Further, young people should be given the opportunity to engage in meaningful collaboration and collective struggle within their communities, so that they can make the difference immediately and into the future as they come to be critically aware of themselves and the important work that needs to be undertaken. Schooling for democracy can become an important driver of this change. However, the change must start now.

On Schooling for Democracy

> We live in difficult and dangerous times—times when precedents lose their significance. If we are content to remain where all is safe and quiet and serene, we shall dedicate ourselves, as teachers have commonly done in the past, to a role of futility, if not of positive social reaction.
>
> *(Counts, 1932, p. 54)*

Counts (1932) wrote about schooling and its role in society almost a century ago, yet the arguments that we live in difficult and dangerous times, and that education can either work towards maintaining the status quo or to build a new social order, have perhaps never been more relevant. Similarly, Dewey (1916) warned against acceptance of the status quo, cautioning that education can either perpetuate social inequality or work towards the reconstruction of society in more equitable and just ways. More recently, Connell (1993) claimed that social justice should be at the heart of education, while Angus (1986) argued that '*all* schools should be committed to principles of equality and justice' (p. 26).

However, despite many progressive education reforms and a large body of critical research into policy and practice over the past century, the goal to build a more inclusive, sustainable and equitable social order seems to be slipping ever further away. Entrenched inequality permeates the entire system, from early childhood learning through to adult and vocational education. School curriculum has become increasingly reductive, as performance on standardised literacy and numeracy tests drives the logic behind school 'reform', removing opportunities for young people to engage in sustained connection with a rich diversity of cultural experiences and learning through the arts, humanities and social sciences. Giroux (2010a) argued that 'under such circumstances rarely do educators ask questions about how schools can prepare students to be informed citizens, nurture a civic imagination, or teach them to be self-reflective about public issues and the world in which they live' (p. 716).

Student performance on standardised literacy and numeracy tests is intimately connected to socioeconomic factors (Riddle, 2018), in which parental education and employment are more significant indicators of schooling success than any teaching or learning that occurs within the classroom. Yet, while it has been evident for decades that rising social and economic inequalities are driving factors of school performance, the policy emphasis has been on increasing accountability for teachers, shifting the discourse from one of equity to one of quality. Such policy moves have responsibilised teachers and students for social and educational inequalities, blaming them rather than the unequal political, economic and social systems and structures under neoliberalised capitalism that ensure that some win and some lose.

The *Alice Springs (Mparntwe) Education Declaration* (Council of Australian Governments Education Council, 2019) was a public commitment by Australian federal, state and territory education ministers to ensure that all Australian students have access to a high-quality education that enables them to become confident and creative, lifelong learners, as well as active and informed members of society. Similarly, the federal US Department of Education's (2021) mission is to promote student achievement and educational excellence, and to ensure equal access for all young people, whereas the UK Department for Education's (2021) vision is to provide world-class education for all young people, 'whatever their background', so that 'everyone has the chance to reach their potential, and live a more fulfilled life' (np).

The policy rhetoric is clear: Education is not simply about providing young people with knowledge and skills to become productive economic units but also the urgent need to provide them with the critical and creative capacities to engage more fully in society. The role of education in liberal democracies such as Australia, the US and the UK has generally involved some commitment to engaging in 'questions about the proper shape and form of democratic education and education for democratic citizenship, but also more philosophical questions about the nature of democracy and the configurations of citizenship within democratic societies' (Biesta, 2013, p. 102). However, questions regarding what democratic education is, how it plays out in practice in classrooms and how schooling might be for democracy remain open to contestation (Sant, 2019).

The civics and citizenship curriculum is one of the ways in which schooling attempts to 'serve its democratic obligations by developing curricula about democracy, loaded with patriotic sentiments and based on a rigid presentation of the nation's governmental institutions that is detached from social, historical and economic patterns' (Smith, 1995, p. 64). However, the curriculum can often be detached from the lived realities of young people, and the structures and form of schooling are themselves often undemocratic, so there can be mixed success from schooling for democracy as it is taught through the formal civics and citizenship curriculum. It is important to note that this book does not present a critique of civics and citizenship curriculum, which plays an important role in teaching young people *about* democracy. However, the intent is to consider schooling at a broader level, as an institutional form of democratic life and participation, rather than offering curriculum suggestions. The project is to seek different forms of schooling that enable and support democracy in the here and now, not as a curriculum offering for citizens-in-waiting or something that happens outside in the world, yet is studied safely within the classroom.

Importantly, schooling should not simply recite an empty rhetoric of democracy—whether that is through curriculum mandates, policy directives or education department mission statements—but should embody the practice of democracy as a lived expression of social becoming and belonging. Gutmann (1999) described democratic education as both a political and educational ideal, through which the principles and practices of democratic citizenry and civic responsibility are formed. This raises important questions regarding who is responsible for teaching young people about democratic behaviours and attitudes, and how a more generative and inclusive notion of civic responsibility can be inculcated (Soder, 1997). Perhaps one response to the question is that offered by Aronowitz and Giroux (1991), who claimed that 'recovering a notion of truth grounded in a critical reading of history that validates and reclaims democratic public life is fundamental to the project of educational reform' (p. 37). For schooling to be for democracy, it first has to consider its own role in the reproduction of inequality. Biesta (2011) claimed that established democracies, such as Australia, the US and UK, seek to 'nurture and maintain interest in and engagement with democratic processes and practices' (p. 5). However, Sant (2019) argued that although mass public schooling has a democratic ethos at its heart, it has become a floating, potentially empty signifier:

> With very limited exceptions, democratic education is claimed to be a normative aspiration guiding the proposals for educational policy and practice of numerous educators. This is particularly significant—democratic

education functions as an entry point for conversations. But as a floating signifier, democratic education is contested.

(p. 679)

At the same time, mass public schooling provides a unique opportunity because of its purpose to provide systematic general education for all students, which is absolutely essential to the purpose and health of democracy (Goodlad, 1979). Prior to the introduction of mass public schooling during the nineteenth and twentieth centuries, most young people were provided with limited access to educational opportunities, with the exception of a small elite. Similarly, most people had limited access to democratic participation. For women, First Nations, Black and other marginalised peoples, the access to education and democratic participation was further limited and then for a longer duration. Indeed, the notion of full participation as a given in democracy and education can really only be traced back to the post-war period in places such as Australia, the UK and US.

Contemporary schools, argued Beane and Apple (2007), 'have a moral obligation to bring the democratic way to life in the culture and curriculum of the school' (p. 8). Such a democratic way of life in the school must be made available to all young people, regardless of their backgrounds or circumstances. Therefore, an education that is for democracy is wholly imbricated with a foundational commitment to social justice. As I have previously argued:

> The principles of democratic education and active citizenship are heavily invested in an understanding of social justice. It is not simply a project of giving the keys to access education to marginalised and disenfranchised young people, but about the project of actively reshaping education in the interests of those least advantaged by the system.
>
> (Riddle & Cleaver, 2017, p. 10)

Schools should be sites in which young people have the opportunity to participate in and shape democratic modes of living and learning together. Rather than being a place of preparation for democratic life, schools are places in which democratic life could, and should, thrive (Dewey, 1916). Aronowitz and Giroux (1987) argued that schools should be democratic public spheres dedicated to self and social empowerment, which requires resistance against forms of schooling that reproduce social and material privilege for the few, while reinforcing inequity for many young people. Taking their argument further, Aronowitz and Giroux (1991) claimed that 'recognizing that there are different voices, languages, histories, and ways of viewing and experiencing the world, and that the recognition and affirmation of these differences is a necessary and important precondition for extending the possibilities of democratic life' (p. 51).

Taking a Deweyan view of schools as places of democratic life, Biesta (2013) considered how the internal democratisation of schooling should be the first step towards a schooling that is for democracy, in which teachers and students have a real interest and stake in the democratic outcomes of their engagements with each other. Dewey (1916) claimed that:

> Society exists through a process of transmission quite as much as biological life. This transmission occurs by means of communication of habits of doing, thinking, and feeling from the older to the younger. Without this communication of ideals, hopes, expectations, standards, opinions, from those members of society who are passing out of the group life to those who are coming into it, social life could not survive. If the members who compose a society lived on continuously, they might educate the new-born members, but it would be a task directed by personal interest rather than social need. Now it is a work of necessity.
>
> *(pp. 3–4)*

However, schooling has often relegated its moral obligation to teach young people about democratic participation and belonging, to instead 'teach conformity to the social, cultural and occupational hierarchy. In our contemporary world, they are not constituted to foster independent thought, let alone encourage independence of thought and action' (Aronowitz, 2008, p. 19). Counts (1932) argued that schools need to be places in which society is formed, rather than simply reflecting the societal status quo or reflecting hegemonic cultural discourses through the curriculum offerings and daily experiences of young people. Schools are active sites of cultural and social formation (Connell, 1993). They are busy places, in which struggles over identity and belonging occur:

> Schools also are part of the cultural apparatus of society in other ways than building (positive or negative) identities. They are key mechanisms in determining what is socially valued as 'legitimate knowledge' and what is seen as merely 'popular'. In helping to define what is legitimate knowledge, they also participate in the process through which particular groups are granted status and other groups remain unrecognised or minimised. Thus, here too schools are at the centre of struggles over a politics of recognition over race/ethnicity, class, gender, sexuality, ability, religion and other important dynamics of power.
>
> *(Apple, 2011, p. 28)*

Schools are also contradictory institutions, replete with ambivalences and tensions. They fulfil pastoral and technical roles for society, through the socialisation, credentialisation and standardisation of young people into the cultural, social, political and economic structures of society. They also reinforce hegemonic logics that flow through social discourses, including along binarised, gendered, raced and classed lines. Schools legitimate particular worldviews, while closing off access to others. Through official and hidden forms of curriculum, young people are enculturated into the practices and ideologies of the present system through their schooling.

At the same time, schools can offer unique opportunities for contestation, difference and recognition. They provide young people with a place in which to participate and learn how to collaborate and collectively struggle towards shared goals through the formation of communal bonds of belonging and becoming. In particular, public schools play a vital role in bringing young people from different backgrounds together, providing an opportunity to collectively live and learn together. Biesta (2020) argued that 'the current crisis has revealed with much clarity how important public education—education funded by public means, accessible to everyone, and accountable to the public—is, particularly for those who only have limited resources of their own' (p. 1). Public schools are a critical element of a democratic society committed to inclusive, caring and sustainable futures through a deep sense of belonging, openness to difference, generative dialogue, supportive public institutions and the development of common bonds.

Overview of This Book

This book considers schooling for democracy during a time of multiple, interconnected global crises. It does so by considering three broad crises in turn before presenting provocations and propositions for a twenty-first century democratic schooling that offers potentially hopeful, sustainable and collective ways of approaching the enormous challenges ahead. Freire (1972) argued that students become increasingly committed to respond to the challenges as they develop more sophisticated understandings and capacities for critical and creative engagement with social problems. Schooling has a unique and vital role to play in providing young people with the means to rise to the complex array of challenges facing them during the twenty-first century. The aim of this book is to consider some of the ways in which schooling might help provide young people with the opportunities to learn how to participate meaningfully and fully in democratic action together.

Chapter 2 considers the contemporary crisis of Western neoliberal–capitalist democracy, with its effects observable in rising social and economic inequalities and the increasing segregation and stratification of schooling systems across much of the contemporary democratic world. The ideological apparatus of the twentieth century—liberalism, capitalism and democracy—has come apart during the first decades of the twenty-first century, precipitating a crisis of democracy. The chapter provides some conceptual and practical encounters with democratic theory and lived experiences, before considering how a new democratic horizon might be possible; one that leaves behind the West's failed project of neoliberalism and moves towards a future horizon of democratic plurality and multiplicity.

Chapter 3 examines the erosion of truth and trust as public commitments against the backdrop of the COVID-19 global pandemic. Drawing on the political theories of Mouffe and Rancière, the chapter considers the rise of populism and neofascist ideologies, alongside the Trump effect on 'alternative facts' and distrust of experts and authority. The destabilisation of public institutions and their role in providing society with public goods has generated a crisis of trust, which has had devastating effects during the pandemic. The chapter considers how schooling for democracy can mitigate and inoculate against the erosion of trust and truth, as well as an examination of the productive potential of dissensus and an agonistic democracy.

Chapter 4 presents an overview of the calamitous effects of climate change, biodiversity reduction and ecosystem destruction, and its precipitation of a public pedagogy, enacted and driven by young people themselves through acts of civil disobedience, resistance and disruption. As examples, the School Strike for Climate protests and the Occupy movement are examined as acts of public resistance that provide potentially hopeful examples of collective action and democratic will as a public pedagogy. The chapter also considers implications for curriculum and pedagogy within the school classroom.

Finally, Chapter 5 draws on the themes and concepts explored throughout the first four chapters to present some propositions for democratic schooling. The question of how schooling can be for democracy is considered within the broader context of a series of multiple and interconnected crises, while recognising that the crises of democracy, populism, trust, climate change and a global pandemic are not exhaustive, and that new crises will continue to emerge even as the current ones are hopefully mitigated or fade from immediacy. In conclusion, the book presents some provocations for teachers, parents, policymakers and the community more broadly, regarding how we might better support and nurture young people through schooling, which enables them to be better prepared to face the challenges ahead.

At the heart of this book is a commitment to public schooling, which is freely accessible to all young people, regardless of their backgrounds or circumstances. Goodlad (1979) contended that public schooling is essential for democratic life, and that although 'schools have too often reflected our shortcomings rather than our ideals is no justification for expecting little of them or doing away with them' (p. 123). If anything, our expectations of schooling need to increase, not in terms of how they perform on standardised tests or other performance metrics, but in terms of how they are situated within the broader public as a site of knowledge-making and active engagement with the world. Giroux (2016) argued that public education is crucial for creating engaged and active citizens who are able to participate meaningfully in democratic societies. As such, teachers need to become citizen–scholars who actively engage with young people in critical dialogue and engagement with the world and its problems, 'providing the conditions for students to have hope and believe that civic life matters and that they *can* make a difference in shaping it so as to expand its democratic possibilities for all groups' (Giroux, 2016, p. xxix).

While democracy is a contested concept, and schools are imperfect institutions, it is within schools that we have the best chance to provide young people with the skills and knowledge to critically and creatively engage with the world in collective and collaborative ways for a more sustainable future. Schooling for democracy gives hope for the future despite the enormous challenges facing humanity and the other living organisms with whom we share this precious, finite planet. As Apple (2011) argued, democratic schooling is not only about schools, but about the kind of society we want and the politics that will get us there. Hopefully, this book offers some useful propositions for how schooling for democracy might enable a more democratic future for all young people, especially those who are marginalised, disenfranchised and cast aside by our present social, economic and political order.

References

Agamben, G. (2011). Introductory note on the concept of democracy. In G. Agamben, A. Badiou, D. Bensaïd, W. Brown, J.-L. Nancy, J. Rancière, K. Ross, & S. Žižek (Eds.), *Democracy in what state?* (pp. 1–5). Columbia University Press.

Amsler, S. S. (2015). *The education of radical democracy*. Routledge.

Angus, L. (1986). *Schooling for social order: Democracy, equality and social mobility in education*. Deakin University Press.

Apple, M. W. (2006). *Educating the 'right' way: Markets, standards, God and inequality* (2nd ed.). Routledge.

Apple, M. W. (2011). Democratic education in neoliberal and neoconservative times. *International Studies in Sociology of Education, 21*(1), 21–31. https://doi.org/10.1080/09620214.2011.543850

Apple, M. W. (2013). *Knowledge, power and education*. Routledge.

Apple, M. W. (2018). *The struggle for democracy in education: Lessons from social realities*. Routledge.

Arblaster, A. (1972). Education and ideology. In D. Rubinstein & C. Stoneman (Eds.), *Education for democracy* (2nd ed., pp. 34–40). Penguin Education.

Arendt, H. (1969). *Between past and future: Eight exercises in political thought*. The Viking Press.

Aronowitz, S. (2008). *Against schooling: Toward an education that matters*. Paradigm Publishers.

Aronowitz, S., & Giroux, H. (1987). *Education under siege: The conservative, liberal and radical debate over schooling*. Routledge & Keegan Paul Ltd.

Aronowitz, S., & Giroux, H. (1991). *Postmodern education: Politics, culture and social criticism*. University of Minnesota Press.

Australian Institute of Health and Welfare. (2021). *Youth detention population in Australia 2020*. https://www.aihw.gov.au/reports/youth-justice/youth-detention-population-in-australia-2020

Bauman, Z. (2017). *Wasted lives: Modernity and its outcasts*. Polity Press.

Beane, J. A., & Apple, M. W. (2007). The case for democratic schools. In M. W. Apple & J. A. Beane (Eds.), *Democratic schools: Lessons in powerful education* (2nd ed., pp. 1–29). Heinemann.

Biesta, G. (2011). *Learning democracy in school and society: Education, lifelong learning, and the politics of citizenship*. Sense Publishers.

Biesta, G. (2013). *The beautiful risk of education*. Routledge.

Biesta, G. (2015). What is education for? On good education, teacher judgement and educational professionalism. *European Journal of Education, 50*(1), 75–87. https://doi.org/10.1111/ejed.12109

Biesta, G. (2020). Have we been paying attention? Educational anaesthetics in a time of crises. *Educational Philosophy and Theory*. https://doi.org/10.1080/00131857.2020.1792612

Bonnor, C., & Shepherd, B. (2016). *Uneven playing field: The state of Australia's schools*. Centre for Policy Development. https://cpd.org.au/2016/05/unevenplayingfield/

Borger, J. (2014, 22 September). Ban Ki-moon: 'World living in an era of unprecedented level of crises'. *The Guardian*. https://www.theguardian.com/world/2014/sep/21/ban-ki-moon-world-living-era-undprecedented-level-crises

Boulianne, S., Lalancette, M., & Ilkiw, D. (2020). 'School Strike 4 Climate': Social media and the international youth protest on climate change. *Media and Communication*, *8*(2), 208–218. https://doi.org/10.17645/mac.v8i2.2768

Bresser-Pereira, L. C. (2010). The global financial crisis and a new capitalism? *Journal of Post Keynesian Economics*, *32*(4), 499–534. https://doi.org/10.2753/PKE0160-3477320401

Brown, W. (2011). 'We are all democrats now…'. In G. Agamben, A. Badiou, D. Bensaïd, W. Brown, J.-L. Nancy, J. Rancière, K. Ross, & S. Žižek (Eds.), *Democracy in what state?* (pp. 44–57). Columbia University Press.

Carr, P. R., & Thésée, G. (2019). *It's not education that scares me, it's the educators: Is there still hope for democracy in education, and education for democracy?* Myers Education Press.

Carr, W., & Hartnett, A. (1996). *Education and the struggle for democracy: The politics of educational ideas*. Open University Press.

Chomsky, N. (2003). *Chomsky on democracy and education* (C. P. Otero, Ed.). RoutledgeFalmer.

Collins, C. (2021, 11 March). Billionaire wealth gains could pay for two-thirds of COVID relief bill. *Inequality.org*. https://inequality.org/great-divide/billionaire-wealth-covid-bill/

Connell, R. W. (1993). *Schools and social justice*. Temple University Press.

Connell, R. W. (2012). Just education. *Journal of Education Policy*, *27*(5), 681–683. https://doi.org/10.1080/02680939.2012.710022

Connell, R. W. (2013). The neoliberal cascade and education: An essay on the market agenda and its consequences. *Critical Studies in Education*, *54*(2), 99–112. https://doi.org/10.1080/17508487.2013.776990

Council of Australian Governments Education Council. (2019). *Alice Springs (Mparntwe) education declaration*. Education Services Australia. http://www.educationcouncil.edu.au/Alice-Springs–Mparntwe–Education-Declaration.aspx

Counts, G. S. (1932). *Dare the school build a new social order?* The John Day Company.

Coy, P. (2021, 10 March). The legacy of the lost year will be devastating inequality. *Bloomberg*. https://www.bloomberg.com/news/articles/2021-03-10/covid-pandemic-made-racial-income-inequality-much-worse

Department for Education. (2021). *About us*. UK Department for Education. https://www.gov.uk/government/organisations/department-for-education/about

Department of Education. (2021). *Mission*. US Department of Education. https://www2.ed.gov/about/overview/mission/mission.html

Dewey, J. (1899). *The school and society: Being three lectures*. University of Chicago Press.

Dewey, J. (1916). *Democracy and education: An introduction to the philosophy of education*. The Macmillan Company.

Doorenspleet, R. (2019). *Rethinking the value of democracy: A comparative perspective*. Palgrave Macmillan.

Dorling, D. (2015). *Injustice: Why social inequality still persists*. Policy Press.

Dorling, D. (2019). *Inequality and the 1%*. Verso.

Extinction Rebellion. (2019). *This is not a drill: An extinction rebellion handbook*. Penguin Books.

Ferrara, A. (2014). *The democratic horizon: Hyperpluralism and the renewal of political liberalism*. Cambridge University Press.

Freire, P. (1972). *Pedagogy of the oppressed*. Penguin Books.
Fukuyama, F. (1989). The end of history? *The National Interest, 16*, 3–18.
Fukuyama, F. (1992). *The end of history and the last man*. The Free Press.
Gardels, N., & Berggruen, N. (2019). *Renovating democracy: Governing in the age of globalization and digital capitalism*. University of California Press.
Giroux, H. A. (2009). *Youth in a suspect society: Democracy or disposability?* Palgrave Macmillan.
Giroux, H. A. (2010a). Rethinking education as the practice of freedom: Paulo Freire and the promise of critical pedagogy. *Policy Futures in Education, 8*(6), 715–721.
Giroux, H. A. (2010b). *Zombie politics and culture in an age of casino capitalism*. Peter Lang.
Giroux, H. A. (2016). *Schooling and the struggle for public life: Democracy's promise and education's challenge* (2nd ed.). Routledge.
Giroux, H. A. (2020, 7 April). The COVID-19 pandemic is exposing the plague of neoliberalism. *Truthout*. https://truthout.org/articles/the-covid-19-pandemic-is-exposing-the-plague-of-neoliberalism/
Goodlad, J. I. (1979). *What schools are for*. Phi Delta Kappa Educational Foundation.
Goodlad, J. I. (1997). Reprise and a look ahead. In J. I. Goodlad & T. J. McMannon (Eds.), *The public purpose of education and schooling* (pp. 155–167). Jossey-Bass Publishers.
Gramsci, A. (1971). *Prison notebooks*. International Publishers.
Gutmann, A. (1999). *Democratic education*. Princeton University Press.
Inman, P. (2021, 2 April). IMF calls for tax hikes on wealthy to reduce income gap. *The Guardian*. https://www.theguardian.com/business/2021/apr/01/imf-tax-wealthy-reduce-income-gap-inequality-covid-crisis
Jones, C., del Pino, J. S., & Mayo, L. (2021). The perfect postnormal storm: COVID-19 chronicles (2020 edition). *World Futures Review*. https://doi.org/10.1177/19467567211027345
Koselleck, R., & Richter, M. W. (2006). Crisis. *Journal of the History of Ideas, 67*(2), 357–400. http://www.jstor.org/stable/30141882
LeGuin, U. K. (1975). The ones who walk away from Omelas. In U. K. LeGuin (Ed.), *The wind's twelve quarters* (pp. 251–259). Bantam Books.
Lipscy, P. Y. (2020). COVID-19 and the politics of crisis. *International Organization, 74*, E98–E127. https://doi.org/10.1017/S0020818320000375
McGregor, G. (2009). Educating for (whose) success? Schooling in an age of neoliberalism. *British Journal of Sociology of Education, 30*(3), 345–358. https://doi.org/10.1080/01425690902812620
McLaren, P., & Farahmandpur, R. (2005). *Teaching against global capitalism and the new imperialism: A critical pedagogy*. Rowman & Littlefield Publishers.
McMannon, T. J. (1997). Introduction: The changing purposes of education and schooling. In J. I. Goodlad & T. J. McMannon (Eds.), *The public purpose of education and schooling* (pp. 1–20). Jossey-Bass Publishers.
Mockler, N. (2014). Simple solutions to complex problems: Moral panic and the fluid shift from 'equity' to 'quality' in education. *Review of Education, 2*(2), 115–143. https://doi.org/10.1002/rev3.3028
Moffitt, B. (2015). How to perform crisis: A model for understanding the key role of crisis in contemporary populism. *Government and Opposition, 50*(2), 189–217. https://doi.org/10.1017/gov.2014.13
Monbiot, G. (2018). *Out of the wreckage: A new politics for an age of crisis*. Verso.
Mouffe, C. (1993). *The return of the political*. Verso.
Mouffe, C. (2019). *For a left populism*. Verso.
Mounk, T. (2018). *The people vs. democracy: Why our freedom is in danger and how to save it*. Harvard University Press.

Nancy, J.-L. (2011). Finite and infinite democracy. In G. Agamben, A. Badiou, D. Bensaïd, W. Brown, J.-L. Nancy, J. Rancière, K. Ross, & S. Žižek (Eds.), *Democracy in what state?* (pp. 58–75). Columbia University Press.

Rancière, J. (2006). *Hatred of democracy*. Verso.

Rancière, J. (2010). *Dissensus: On politics and aesthetics.* Continuum.

Riddle, S. (2018). Resisting educational inequity and the 'bracketing out' of disadvantage in contemporary schooling. In S. Gannon, W. Sawyer, & R. Hattam (Eds.), *Resisting educational inequality: Reframing policy and practice in schools serving vulnerable communities* (pp. 17–30). Routledge.

Riddle, S. (2019). Democracy and education in local–global contexts. *The International Education Journal: Comparative Perspectives, 18*(1), 1–6.

Riddle, S., & Apple, M. W. (2019). Education and democracy in dangerous times. In S. Riddle & M. W. Apple (Eds.), *Re-imagining education for democracy* (pp. 1–9). Routledge.

Riddle, S., & Cleaver, D. (2017). *Alternative schooling, social justice and marginalised students.* Palgrave Macmillan.

Riddle, S., & Heffernan, A. (2018). Education and democracy for complex contemporary childhoods. *Global Studies of Childhood, 8*(4), 319–324. https://doi.org/10.1177/2043610618817370

Rodin, J. (2015). *Remarks by Dr. Judith Rodin at the Cities for Tomorrow Conference.* https://www.rockefellerfoundation.org/news/remarks-by-dr-judith-rodin-at-the-cities-for-tomorrow-conference/

Sant, E. (2019). Democratic education: A theoretical review (2006–2017). *Review of Educational Research, 89*(5), 655–696. https://doi.org/10.3102/0034654319862493

Sardar, Z. (2010). Welcome to postnormal times. *Futures, 42*(5), 435–444. https://doi.org/10.1016/j.futures.2009.11.028

Sardar, Z., & Sweeney, J. A. (2016). The three tomorrows of postnormal times. *Futures, 75*, 1–13. https://doi.org/10.1016/j.futures.2015.10.004

Smith, H. (1995). It's education for, not about, democracy. *Educational Horizons, 73*(2), 62–69.

Soder, R. (1997). Democracy: Do we really want it? In J. I. Goodlad & T. J. McMannon (Eds.), *The public purpose of education and schooling* (pp. 85–96). Jossey-Bass Publishers.

Taylor, T. (2013). Neoconservative progressivism, knowledgeable ignorance and the origins of the next history war. *History Australia, 10*(2), 227–240. https://doi.org/10.1080/14490854.2013.11668469

Voltolini, B., Natorski, M., & Hay, C. (2020). Introduction: The politicisation of permanent crisis in Europe. *Journal of European Integration, 42*(5), 609–624. https://doi.org/10.1080/07036337.2020.1792460

Wells, H. G. (1922). *The outline of history: Being a plain history of life and mankind.* The Macmillan Company.

2
IS THIS THE END OF THE DEMOCRATIC DREAM?

Introduction

> Capitalism is proving itself weak at the very point where its champions have thought it impregnable. It is failing to meet the pragmatic test; it no longer works; it is unable even to organize and maintain production. In its present form capitalism is not only cruel and inhuman; it is also wasteful and inefficient. It has exploited our natural resources without the slightest regard for the future needs of our society; it has forced technology to serve the interests of the few rather than the many; it has chained the engineer to the vagaries and inequities of the price system; it has plunged the great nations of the earth into a succession of wars ever more devastating and catastrophic in character; and only recently it has brought on a world crisis of such dimensions that the entire economic order is paralyzed.
>
> (Counts, 1932, pp. 47–48)

All around, an abundance of evidence points to the erosion of the pillars of contemporary society—liberalism, capitalism and democracy. The triumphant heralding of the end of history in the late-twentieth century has been followed by the collapse of the very social, economic and political apparatuses that sustained the liberal–democratic geopolitical order. Rising anti-democratic sentiment in many parts of the globe has borne out in the erosion of democratic ideals, civil rights and the social contract. Authoritarian, neofascist and populist movements are in the ascendant, while distrust of government, science and rationality have precipitated a toxic mix of contemporary forces that threaten to render democracy unusable right at a critical moment in human history.

Economic and social inequalities are on the rise, with obscene levels of wealth concentrated in the hands of the very few, while many people live well below the poverty line in countries that are ranked among the most advanced economies in the world. Tensions are high, and social unrest is growing, as the allure of the promised capitalist utopia wears thin. However, there seems at the present time to be limited scope for re-imagining, let alone replacing, the current systems of political and economic reason that drive much of the policymaking and contemporary public discourse. Inertia is a powerful force, and perhaps one of the most successful outcomes of the neoliberal agenda has been to render the idea of something different as being unthinkable.

Yet, think differently we must if we are to survive—let alone thrive—in the coming years and decades. Clearly, business as usual cannot continue indefinitely. The premise of continual growth and wealth accumulation has wreaked havoc on the natural systems of the planet, as more things are dug from the earth, bulldozed over or dragnetted from the oceans, to satisfy the inexhaustible demands of a global consumerist economy, which requires an endless chain of production and consumption. We are killing ourselves and many other species with whom we share the planet, poisoning the lands and waterways, and wreaking destruction on a global scale that will require many generations to heal.

This chapter considers the broader contours of the failures of neoliberalism as the contemporary policy ideology within liberal–democratic societies during the first decades of the twenty-first century, to better understand how intimately the popular notion of contemporary democracy is entirely meshed with a Western, capitalist, neoliberal sensibility. The current crisis of democracy is contextualised within a broader set of challenges, including rising social and economic inequalities, social unrest and the inability or unwillingness, for public institutions and democratic systems to create meaningful change. Some consideration is given to possibilities of a new democratic horizon, which is more sustainable and collective. In doing so, key threads regarding how schooling might be for democracy are described.

Whose Democracy Is It Anyway?

Despite its widespread uptake in political governance, democracy is not a natural state of affairs, nor is it some kind of end-point of human history. Unhelpfully, 'discussions on democracy often result in platitudinous affirmations that it is naturally desirable, and, as a corollary, anything that is not democratic is considered virtually irrelevant' (Carr, 2008, p. 148). Smith (1995) argued that, although not a natural instinct, democracy 'is an imaginative, constructive approach to government that seeks to make the most of human potential, while reducing some of the worst inclinations toward predatory behaviors' (p. 67). Similarly, Arendt (1969) claimed that when democracies are fully realised—raising of course the question of whether there have been any examples of societies in which fully realised democracy has been achieved—deception of the public cannot occur without a willing and enthusiastic self-deception. Contemporary partisan politics in the US perhaps provides one illustration of the power of enthusiastic self-deception by a population convinced of its own political infallibility.

At the heart of democracy is the ideal of the society of equals (Frega, 2019), in which radical equality is ensured, difference is celebrated as an affirming force and the contribution of each person to the common good is celebrated (Schostak, 2019). While Rancière (2006) claimed that equality was the basis of the democratic encounter, 'elites see equality as a danger' (Schostak, 2019, p. 1103). This is nothing new. During the interwar period, Counts (1932) warned that 'if democracy is to be achieved in the industrial age, powerful classes must be persuaded to surrender their privileges, and institutions deeply rooted in popular prejudice will have to be radically modified or abolished. ... Ruling classes never surrender their privileges voluntarily' (pp. 50–51).

There are many countries in the world that call themselves democracies, although the term has been used rather loosely in some instances. Just because one lives in a society that describes itself as democratic and has a constitution, institutions and laws that permit the use of democratic processes does not guarantee their full realisation. Democracy can be understood as society's attempt to balance individual and collective freedoms with individual and collective responsibilities (Goodlad, 1997). When the balance shifts in favour of one or the other, then democracy cannot be fully realised.

One of the biggest issues with democracy is that it can become a sliding signifier, much like the concept of freedom, which enables its take-up and mobilisation by different groups with vastly divergent interests (Apple, 2004). For example, the democracy envisaged by environmental protest groups, such as the Extinction Rebellion movement, sits in stark contrast to the tightly controlled public relation activities of political parties in an election cycle. Similarly, the type of democracy advocated by leftist progressives with a desire for increased collaboration, social cohesion and welfare supports for society's disadvantaged and marginalised, sits opposite the desires of globalised corporate elites for a compliant and distracted electorate. Fully realised democracy, in which the people have agency over deliberative decision-making and the public institutions that govern their lives, is viewed as being dangerous to the status quo. Indeed, 'democracy is increasingly viewed as a dangerous concept and an even more dangerous practice' (Riddle & Apple, 2019, p. 3).

Carr (2010) argued that 'the epistemology of democracy is laden with normative values about the meaning of freedom, justice, liberty, fairness, and empowerment' (p. 30). Yet, these value-laden concepts are also open to wide interpretation by different groups. They have never been impartial, but always deployed to serve the interests—of generally more powerful groups—of those within societies who seek to gain or sustain power over others. Equality and freedom are taken to be the bedrock principles of democracy, yet there has never been a situation in which all those within a society are treated equally or have commensurate freedoms. One example from recent history is the long struggle of the women's rights movements around the world, through which twentieth century feminism made important gains in gender equality and the representation of women in education, the workplace and public life. However, despite these gains, women continue to be underrepresented in key leadership positions and are denied a truly representative voice. When one considers the intersections of race and class with gender, the picture becomes even more bleak.

Additionally, Frega (2019) claimed that we need to take a wide view of democracy, which arises from the successful integration of relational parity, inclusive authority and social involvement within the broader political sphere. This requires the inclusion of all people, rather than a select political class or corporate elite, including meaningful engagement with minority groups and other marginalised people within society. To have a society in which there remain 'wasted lives' (Bauman, 2017) is to accept a limited view of democracy, more akin to the strict criteria for citizenship in ancient Athens—supported by an exclusionary politics bounded by gender, class and cultural identity—than a healthy, functioning twenty-first century democracy. Garton Ash (2020) argued that we need to reconceive liberalism to better defend liberal values and institutions against threats from populists and authoritarians, removing the one-dimensional economic liberalism, which he described as dogmatic market fundamentalism, and by rising to meet the global challenges of the twenty-first century.

In their introduction to *Democratic Schools: Lessons in Powerful Education* (Apple & Beane, 2007), Beane and Apple (2007) argued that the values and principles of democracy included a commitment to the common good, concern for the dignity and rights of minorities, the welfare of others, the open sharing of ideas, critical reflection and engagement with each other, plus the creation of social institutions that defend and extend democratic life. Similarly, Fielding and Moss (2010) claimed that democracy in practice should be understood as the multiple and diverse ways in which people living in communities and societies can think, be and act in relation with each other. Over a century ago, Dewey (1916) also argued that democratic virtue arises through the act of living with each other with a view to the collective good of society, rather than some small-minded individualistic possessiveness of freedom and power.

Clearly, what we call democracies writ large—that is, the machinations of our political institutions, electoral systems and governments—fall well short of the ideals of democracy as a commitment to equality and freedom of all within a society. However, that does not mean that democracy does not exist in some form. Perhaps one of the most promising examples of democratic practice in a commitment to freedom and equality can be observed in contemporary activist and grassroots organisations and experiences, 'especially in social movements aimed at promoting economic and racial justice, from the civil rights movement in the United States to the battle to end apartheid in South Africa' (Taylor, 2019, p. 29). As Rancière (2006) explained, democracy is found in the encounters between equals, and these movements offer the chance for people to collectively express their political will in multiple and diverse ways. Chapter 3 explores some of the productive encounters of democratic expression by young people through collective action, civil disobedience, disruption and refusal of the hegemonic order.

The erosion of democratic virtues through the rise of the globalised corporate elites and the enablement of these powerful oligarchic interests by the political class through neoliberal policymaking in many contemporary Westernised liberal democracies have reduced democracy to a minimal form (Markell, 2010), expressed through the electoral cycle and voting this party or that party into power, with little difference between them. It is evident that this procedural approach to a minimalist democracy 'is a recipe not for democratic equality but for aggression and exploitation' (Dallmayr, 2017, p. 13). Further, Mouffe (1993) made the prescient argument that liberal democracy would become more aligned with the realities of liberal–democratic capitalism, under which democracy is relegated to an electoral set piece rather than a fully realised mode of collective life. Under such circumstances, Mouffe (1993) cautioned that those who were excluded from access and participation could become attracted to antiliberal and populist forces. The US context during the lead-up to the 2016 Presidential election and subsequent social instability is an example of the effects of capitalism overriding democracy.

There is a tension at the heart of democracy, in which liberalism and capitalism work both with and against the other. Liberalism, concerned with a fundamental commitment to freedom and equality, becomes distorted through the technologies of capitalism, rendering a neoliberalism that promotes a thin version of democracy as represented by choice within markets and a possessive individualism, rather than a thick democracy, which emphasises self-rule, equality and participation in decision-making and access to forms of social, political and economic power within the polity (Swift, 2002). While democracy can be used to support arguments about the importance of human rights, freedom, inclusion and equity, democracy can also be used to further arguments for increased control by corporate elites and the political class in the name of open and free markets and the primacy of consumer choice. For example, 'freedom of the kind championed by neoliberals means freedom from competing interests. It means freedom from the demands of social justice, from environmental constraints, from collective bargaining and from the taxation that funds public services. It means, in sum, freedom from democracy' (Monbiot, 2016, p. 12).

Rancière (2010) claimed that democracy presents a paradox because it is neither truly a form of government nor a form of social life, but what he called an 'institution of politics'. The answer to where power of rule is grounded within the community 'is an astonishing one: namely, that the very ground for the power of ruling is that there is no ground at all' (Rancière, 2010, p. 50). Bensaïd (2011) was less forgiving in the assessment that 'the self-contradiction and ambivalence of the democratic pretension have been thrown into strong relief by the pressure of liberal globalization' (p. 21). Indeed, contemporary democracy has been described as a merger of corporate and state power (Brown, 2011), in which the state outsources many of its functions, such as the military, prisons, hospitals and schools. Finance capital and globalised trading in stocks and futures have more influence over fiscal and social policy than the needs of the people within society. The revolving door of politics, lobbying and corporate board membership is well entrenched in most liberal–democratic societies, in which the lines between government and enterprise have blurred to the point of becoming indistinguishable.

Globalisation has exacerbated already existing issues with the social fabric and democracy's place within the social, economic and political structures and institutions of contemporary liberal–democratic societies. Yet, the divide between the rich and poor predates the globalisation movement of the twentieth century, and the class conflict is built into capitalism (just ask Marx!). However, just because class conflict and inequality seem baked into contemporary capitalist societies, it does not mean that democracy is impossible, but it is more challenging, given that inequality fundamentally undermines the principle of political and social equality (Taylor, 2019) that forms the bedrock of democracy. Amsler (2015) claimed that capitalism in isolation was not the problem, 'but its intersection with forces of dehumanizing and parameterizing power that close possibilities for difference, dialogue, intervention and resistance' (p. 35).

On democracy's promise of equality, Brown (2011) argued that modern democracies have never really worked on the premise of equality beyond the formal representation of one vote per person in elections and officially receiving equal treatment under the law. Of course, this is open to debate, given how easily those with substantial financial resources are able to manipulate the legal process to their advantage, whether by hiring the 'best' legal representation, settling disputes in out-of-court agreements that involve vast sums of money, or being able to draw on networks of political and legal influence from their networks. Coming up against the machinery of the legal system is a vastly different proposition for the working class and those living in poverty and marginalised contexts.

According to Carey (1995), the twentieth century was characterised by three key political developments in Western, liberalised countries: 'the growth of democracy, the growth of corporate power, and the growth of corporate propaganda as a means of protecting corporate power against democracy' (p. 18). The last point is particularly salient, given that current liberal–democratic states like Australia, the UK and US resemble corporate oligarchies more than democratic societies, in which corporate benefactors 'donate' to political campaigns to ensure influence over policy decisions. Two immediately obvious examples are the gun lobby, spearheaded by the National Rifle Association in the US, and the mining lobby, including multinational behemoths like Rio Tinto and BHP in Australia. Carey's (1995) analysis found that corporate propaganda has been effective in controlling and deflecting the democratic purposes of elections to ensure that corporate interests are served ahead of the needs of communities, especially those who are marginalised and disenfranchised from the flows of power and capital within society.

Schostak and Goodson (2020) claimed that the absence of democracy from the daily lives of people enables the concentration of political power within a small elite group, which is supported by increased sophistication in the technologies of surveillance and platform capitalism. The combined effect of social media and widespread digital surveillance works to ensure that the masses are kept distracted by a non-stop feed of consumption and spectacle, while wealth and power continue to be siphoned away from the vast majority of people (Zuboff, 2019). It could be argued that 'modern society is the propaganda society dependent upon a largely acquiescent public who are to be "educated" to the current social problems and the elite's desired solution to them' (Schostak & Goodson, 2020, p. 7). Rancière (2006) was particularly unforgiving in his assessment of the contemporary democratic subject, for whom politics is forgotten and the individuation is subjugated to a system of capitalist domination that renders them an 'idiotic consumer of popcorn, reality TV, safe sex, social security, the right to difference, and anticapitalist or "alterglobalist" illusions' (p. 89).

There is a clear threat posed to those who have access to wealth, power and privilege in contemporary capitalist democratic societies is the threat of democracy itself (Rancière, 2006). The aim is to avoid 'too much democracy' as a cultural and political problem (Apple, 2006). As such, only safe and controllable forms of democracy are to be permitted, which do not destabilise the status quo or provide alternative propositions to the political and economic order. Thus, we have a representative form of democracy that nods towards the principles of equality and liberty, yet ensure the continuation of entrenched power structures, political parties, policymakers and political advisers. It seems little wonder that wealth and power continue to accumulate in the hands of an elite few when 'equality is repressed in contemporary individualist views of representative market democracies' (Schostak & Goodson, 2020, p. 11).

During elections, politicians will gesture to the idealised version of democratic society, imploring the electorate to buy their vision of a brighter, more prosperous future. However, when they are outside of the electoral market machine, such political representatives revert back to the mode of serving the interests of the elite, whether by murky links between key political donors and the development of policy platforms and legislative agendas, or the revolving doors of political lobbying, representative politics and corporate boardrooms. Bauman's (2004) critique of such behaviour laid claim to political leaders washing their hands of the misfortunes of those whom they purport to represent, thus exposing the lie of a representative democratic system. In place of a genuine democratic commitment to society by its leaders, 'citizens are now abandoned to their own cunning and guts while held solely responsible for the results of their struggles against adversities not of their making' (Bauman, 2004, p. 65). Further, despite claims of having choice within the marketplaces of education, work and life more broadly, 'individuals are neither invited nor encouraged to think of the conditions under which their life purposes are pursued—let alone to contribute to their revision and reform' (Bauman, 2004, p. 65).

Clearly, contemporary societies that purport to be liberal capitalist democracies have found themselves in a situation in which they are not especially democratic. Instead of a thick democracy, many offer only a thin version, with a veneer of liberalism and the notion of equality, so long as it does not come into contestation with the sustained political power of elites. Instead of becoming a lived reality for peoples around the world, democracy seems instead to have become a political 'horizon', which has enabled the rise of neo-oligarchic powers and provided fertile grounds for populism and antipolitical attitudes to ferment (Ferrara, 2014). Further, the infiltration of the market into all aspects of social, political and economic life has seen the increase of control over everyday life by non-democratic practices and institutions (Schostak & Goodson, 2020).

Democracy in Trouble

There are many examples of the enormous range of pressures faced by contemporary formations of democracy, ranging from the increasing polarisation of politics in the US and the rise of Trumpism, the fallout from Brexit in the UK, increasing social and economic inequalities and rising dissatisfaction with the political class in places like Australia, the growing reach of neofascist and ultra-right-wing conservatism across Europe, all the way to the collapse of fledgling and struggling democracies in Asia and South America.

Despite its apparent taken-for-grantedness, the versions of democracy that presently exist in contemporary societies are neither politically stable nor particularly democratic. For example, the free, rational subject at the heart of liberalism presupposes democracy as the only truly legitimate contemporary political form, which has become incontestable despite the perpetuation of Whiteness, masculinity and colonisation as driving factors of contemporary Western democracy, and their attendant hierarchies, exclusions and violences committed upon others (Brown, 2011). From the second half of the twentieth century, global engagement has been marked by the imperialist war machinery of the US as it exported a particular version of democracy to the world; first, in Korea and Vietnam, then to Bosnia and Serbia, before turning its attention to Iraq and Afghanistan. Increasingly, the military focus of Western democracies, led by the US, has been turned on China, which has been flexing its considerable maritime supremacy in the South China Sea and more broadly. The recent announcement of the AUKUS (Australia–United Kingdom–United States) alliance, with a promise by the two nuclear powered states to provide Australia with state-of-the-art nuclear submarines, not only had the desired effect of aggravating China and harking back to something reminiscent of Anglosphere alliances from the early twentieth century, but also managed to create a significant rift with France, which is a leading power in the EU (Conley & Green, 2021).

However, the external pressures of delicate geopolitics, protecting the economic interests of nation-states and navigating tense international maritime security issues pale against the internal pressures facing democracies—both well-established and fledgling democracies—across the world. For example, Mouffe (1999) argued that liberal–democratic societies are poorly equipped to address the growing challenge of right-wing extremism and political disaffection due to their reliance on a notion of the individualistic, universalistic and rationalistic democratic subject. The issue with the emphasis on the individual over the collective is that it 'erases the dimension of the political and impedes envisaging in an adequate manner the nature of a pluralistic democratic public sphere' (Mouffe, 1999, p. 745). Two decades on from Mouffe's writing, the state of political disenfranchisement and disaffection has grown markedly worse, and the rising tide of neofascistic and right-wing populist demagogues has become a clear and present danger for democratic institutions and governance.

One example of the perilous state of democracies can be observed in the destabilisation of US democratic institutions during the Trump presidency, which culminated in a violent mob of armed insurgents rioting and attempting to storm the US Capitol building on 6 January 2021 in an attempt to overturn Trump's electoral defeat. The violence of the mob was unmistakable, with footage of the attack livestreamed around the world. Five people died either during or shortly after the attack, 138 police officers were injured, and in the eight months following the attack, four responding police officers had taken their own lives (Wild et al., 2021). However, the most remarkable aspect of the attack was Trump's (alleged) incitement of the attack. His actions and words in the lead-up to, during and following the events of 6 January 2021, have been described as a reckless and dangerous normalisation of political violence (Bump, 2021). The refusal of Trump and his supporters to acknowledge electoral defeat, followed by a concerted effort to overturn the results through legal challenges, threats and appeals to state legislatures, and finally the instigation of the mob attack on the Capitol, have been described as nothing short of an attempted coup (Boot, 2021).

During the course of his presidency, Trump incited violence on several occasions through posts made to his Twitter account (Cathey & Keneally, 2020), which eventually led to his permanent exclusion by the social media platform, although arguably long past the point of achieving anything useful to ensuring the integrity of democratic institutions and conventions in the US. Even prior to Trump's presidency, Street (2015) argued that 'the contemporary United States may not be a fascist state. But this hardly means it deserves to be considered anything like a genuine democracy' (p. 6). The US has long witnessed the fermenting of extremist right-wing groups, including White supremacists, neo-Nazis, conspiracy theorists, armed nationalistic militia and anti-immigration activists. They share common bonds based on hate, fear and exclusion of the other, with racist, sexist and ableist views of a homogenous, hierarchical society in which certain people (i.e., White men) have supremacy over all other groups. Perhaps Street (2015) put it most bluntly, claiming that the US:

> Is neither a dictatorship nor a democracy. It is something in between or perhaps difference altogether: a corporate-managed state-capitalist

pseudo-democracy that sells the narrow interests of the wealthy business and financial elite as the public interest, closes off critical and independent thought, and subjects culture, politics, policy, institutions, the environment, daily life, and individual minds to the often hidden and unseen authoritarian dictates of money and profit. It is a corporate and financial plutocracy whose managers generally prefer to rule through outwardly democratic and noncoercive means since leading American corporations and their servants have worked effectively at draining and disabling democracy's radical and progressive potential by propagandizing, dulling, pacifying, deadening, overextending, overstressing, atomizing, and demobilizing the citizenry. At the same time, American state and capitalist elites remain ready, willing, and able to maintain their power with the help from ever more sinister and sophisticated methods and tools of repression, brutality, and coercive control.

(pp. 5–6)

Following the turbulence of the 2020 US presidential election, there have been numerous challenges to the electoral outcomes, and a concerningly high number of Republican voters and Trump supporters continue to assert that the election was rigged and that Trump remains the rightful president. Such an argument seems more comfortable coming from tin pot dictators than from US presidents, yet Trump continues to assert that he rightfully won the 2020 election and that it was stolen from him. He is not alone in those views. Almost two-thirds (55 per cent) of Republicans believed that there was widespread voter fraud in the 2020 US presidential elections (Cox, 2021). There are disturbing elements of proto-fascism gaining ground in the US, and the increasing social and economic divisions, polarising political ideologies and cultural inwardness do not portend well for the coming years and decades.

Despite claiming multiple times that he intends to run again for the US presidency in 2024, a more likely situation could arise in which the complex set of Republican state-based voter suppression tactics, gerrymandering of electoral boundaries and increased rejection of democratic norms and conventions will further erode public confidence in the electoral process in the upcoming 2022 federal mid-term elections. As Monbiot (2020) warned, the fundamental divisions within the US make it ripe for a more competent autocrat to take control in the near future, despite the momentary reprieve for democratic conventions during the Biden presidency. Tufekci (2020) went further, to argue that 'make no mistake: the attempt to harness Trumpism—without Trump, but with calculated, refined, and smarter political talent—is coming' (np). Time will tell how things play out in the US, but there is no doubt that the state of US democracy is tenuous, with significant global economic, social and political implications yet to be fully realised. While the US becoming a full-blown fascist state is neither imminent nor certain, 'the latent conditions for the actualization of fascism are everywhere in evidence, something that could be called a dormant fascism waiting to erupt' (McLaren & Farahmandpur, 2005, p. 5). As such, the threat to a democratic future in the US is very real and something that should not be taken lightly.

Moving from the US to South Asia, Myanmar provides a compelling case study of the failed promise of neoliberal capitalist democracy. Following decades of military rule, Myanmar began a transition from authoritarianism to democracy in 2011. However, the reform process faced significant hurdles, including limits on civic and political freedom, economic liberalisation and sectarian conflict, which was clearly evidenced in the continued political power of the military and the lack of will or capability of the elected party to peacefully resolve ongoing conflicts in Rakhine State and the ethnic cleansing of Rohingyas (Stoke & Aung, 2020). A couple of years into the democratisation project, it was apparent that the challenges to creating a sustained democratic peace were significant, and that liberal democratisation would not provide a lasting solution without equitable political representation and self-determination for minority groups within Myanmar (Nilsen, 2013).

The appalling treatment of the Rohingya has received widespread international condemnation (BBC News, 2020). In August 2017, the Myanmar military undertook a campaign of ethnic cleansing against Rohingya Muslims in Rakhine State, which Aung San Suu Kyi—a Nobel Peace Prize laureate—repeatedly denied was an act of genocide. The International Court of Justice (2020) ruled that Myanmar was required to take emergency measures to prevent the persecution and killing of Rohingya. By 2019, hope was fading for democracy in Myanmar, and in the de factor leader of the National League for Democracy, Aung San Suu Kyi, as dissenters were imprisoned on spurious grounds, protests disbanded and the military brazenly sought to quell any civic disturbance or criticism (Hoekstra, 2019). After securing an electoral victory in November 2020, the National League for Democracy introduced regressive laws to prevent media reporting on the conflict in Rakhine State and ethnic cleansing of the Rohingya population by the military, alongside growing authoritarianism and civic repression (Mun, 2021).

Then, on 1 February 2021, the Myanmar military seized power from the National League for Democracy, detained Aung San Suu Kyi and other political leaders in a series of early morning raids, and declared a one-year state of emergency, which has since been extended. The coup was immediately met with widespread international condemnation and increased international legal proceedings against Myanmar rulers and military (Renshaw, 2021). Alarmingly, over 125,000 school teachers and 19,500 university staff in Myanmar have since been suspended by the military junta for joining a civil disobedience movement that opposed the military coup (Reuters, 2021a). Despite ongoing condemnation of the military's repressive tactics, at the present time, there appears to be limited chance of an outcome that supports and enables democracy within Myanmar. In addition to the military coup and repressive tactics, Myanmar has also experienced catastrophic effects from the COVID-19 pandemic, including a failed health system, underreporting of cases and deaths, plus the constant threat of violence and detention faced by health workers who oppose the regime (Ratcliffe, 2021).

Moving to the Middle East, Syrian President Bashar al-Assad won a fourth seven-year term on 26 May 2021, with 95.1 per cent of the vote, in an election described as fraudulent by France, Germany, Italy, the UK and US (Reuters, 2021b). The win came after a decade of conflict, which has caused the displacement of over 11 million people and the deaths of hundreds of thousands, including through the alleged use of chemical weapons ordered by Assad (Hubbard, 2020). The situation has been described as one of the worst humanitarian crises in history, with displaced children living in insecure and impoverished conditions, in which they are 'exposed to various forms of exploitation, from child labor to sexual violence, to recruitment and employment by armed and criminal groups' (Berti, 2015, p. 43). In the past decade, approximately 5 million Syrian children have been born into conflict, with little access to schooling or healthcare. The harmful effects on Syria's future will last for generations.

In Europe, authoritarian 'illiberal' Belarusian President Alexander Lukashenko was returned to power in August 2020, with 80 per cent of the vote, amid claims of widespread fraud and vote tampering (Roth & Auseyushkin, 2020). A wave of protests and civil unrest followed the election, with security forces violently suppressing dissent, including the arrest and torture of thousands of citizens, including journalists, activists and political opposition figures (Human Rights Watch, 2021). Amnesty International (2020) claimed that the widespread human rights abuses and torture suggested that the violent repression had been sanctioned at the highest level. On 23 May 2021, Ryanair flight FR4978 was diverted to Minsk, escorted by a Belarusian military MiG fighter jet. Upon landing, prominent opposition activist, Roman Protasevich was detained by Belarusian authorities, who released a forced confession video the following day. The incident prompted widespread condemnation as a 'State-sponsored hijacking' and international airlines began to avoid Belarusian airspace (Ziady, 2021). However, with the support of Russia, Lukashenko stared down international criticism and claimed that the country was under a coordinated 'hybrid attack' by its opponents (Ilyushina, 2021).

Belarus has long been considered to be an illiberal democracy in a state of 'near-tyranny' (Zakaria, 1997), although recent events suggest that the Belarusian people have reached a crisis point in their struggles for a more democratic future. Among other groups protesting the regime, teachers have been singled out by Lukashenko, who declared that all teachers must support the state ideology, which was followed by widespread teacher strikes and resignations (Makhovsky, 2020). Instead of being in schools and universities, students have been at the centre of the protests and civil disobedience, with serious risks to their personal safety (Nepogodin, 2020).

The UK is also in the middle of a major shift in its political, economic and social makeup. As the birthplace of contemporary parliamentary democracy and the much-lauded Westminster system, the UK appears to be at risk of breaking apart, for the first time in more than two centuries. While it is easy to lay the blame for the current instability on the UK's withdrawal from the European Union (i.e., Brexit), there are much deeper currents at play that threaten the future of a unified and democratic UK. Perhaps the most damaging force, which was a direct and indirect influence on the toxic politics of Brexit is rising social and economic inequalities. Dallmayr (2017) argued that in itself, economic inequality is neither new nor particularly harmful. Instead, the penetration of inequality into political and public life is what creates the divisive and exclusionary tactics of contemporary inequality, which permeates across all spheres of public and private life.

One example of rising inequality can be observed in the increase in people experiencing regular food insecurity, which rose from 27.7 per cent in 2014 to 45.8 per cent in 2016 for adults on low incomes (Loopstra et al., 2019). While real wages have stagnated over the past decade, the cost of living has continued to increase, which has put increased pressure on particular groups of people, including those living in poverty, with disabilities, minority groups and other disadvantaged groups. At the other end of the economic spectrum are the wealthy elites, whose share of wealth has rapidly expanded over the same time, and even accelerated during the COVID pandemic. Dorling (2019) warned that, as inequality widens, there are significant negative effects on social cohesion and a sense of civic responsibility to each other:

> When a society becomes as unequal as the UK now is, avarice rises. As inequalities increase, people already at the top become ever more motivated solely by greed. The source of inequality is a failure to control the greedy. Often they feel that they need more money despite all their wealth. They are made to feel that way because status and respect are increasingly measured in purely financial terms.
>
> (p. 146)

Much of the politics of resentment that drove the Brexit debate was fuelled by the frustration and estrangement of those who had been left behind in the race to accumulate individual wealth and resources at the expense of the public good. Aslam (2017) described the experience of social estrangement and devitalisation of marginalised and disenfranchised people as being intricately tied to the actions of powerful corporations and political elites, which operate in their own interests without any meaningful public accountability. Further, Ferrara (2014) explained that there is a de-democratisation effect that flows from globalised capitalism and the role of financial markets in creating inhospitable conditions for democratic participation and engagement. As such, it is little wonder that a politics of resentment was so easy manipulated during the lead-up to the Brexit vote in 2016. Such politics have continued to fester, generating increased levels of political withdrawal and rejection of the systems and institutions that have, until now, held the UK together. The roots of the current social and economic woes in the UK can be directly traced back to the neoliberal policies made by the Thatcher government during the 1980s, and the flow-on effects of those policy enactments are still being felt today in the crisis facing contemporary UK democracy.

The Neoliberalisation of Democracy

Monbiot (2018) argued that the second half of the twentieth century could be described as a political conflict between the ideologies of social democracy and neoliberalism. Despite there being some examples of relatively successful capitalist social democracies in the Scandinavian countries of Finland, Norway, Sweden and Denmark, in the main, neoliberalism has been the key driver for economic and social policymaking in many capitalist liberal democracies around the world, especially in the EU and Anglophone countries. Further, McChesney (1999) claimed that:

> To be effective, democracy requires that people feel a connection to their fellow citizens, and that this connection manifests itself through a variety of nonmarket organizations and institutions. A vibrant political culture needs community groups, libraries, public schools, neighborhood organizations, cooperatives, public meeting places, voluntary associations, and trade unions to provide ways for citizens to meet, communicate, and interact with their fellow citizens. Neoliberal democracy, with its notion of the market uber alles, takes dead aim at this sector. Instead of communities, it produces shopping malls. The net result is an atomized society of disengaged individuals who feel demoralized and socially powerless.
>
> (p. 11)

Neoliberal ideology seeks to place 'the market' at the centre of all human endeavour, with a particular emphasis on the spheres of politics and economics. However, even education has been increasingly subjected to neoliberal policymaking over the past three to four decades. Key practices of neoliberal policymaking include privatisation—through which public services and institutions are given over to private, for-profit interests and corporations in the name of efficiency and service return—and marketisation—through which everything is made subject to the machinations of a free market system, complete with supply and demand, market logics and rationalities. The key movement away from a Keynesian economy happened during the last two decades of the twentieth century, and is perhaps best exemplified through the leadership and policies under the Thatcher government in the UK, the Keating government in Australia and the Reagan administration in the US. However, subsequent political leaders of all persuasions in many countries around the world have continued down the path of privatisation and marketisation well into the twenty-first century, to the point where:

> Democracy itself becomes a commodity to be bought and sold in the education market, packaged up and distributed by corporations who provide for-profit education in the form of ventures such as online charter schools, marketed to parents as a more democratic, personalised and accessible educational opportunity for their children.
>
> *(Riddle & Heffernan, 2018, p. 321)*

Importantly, neoliberalism focuses on the individual as being the centre of political and economic activity, rather than the collective. Therefore, all public services and spaces are recast as individual services and spaces. As one example, schooling goes from being a site of education for living in the world and preparation for meaningful civic engagement in society, to one in which an individual seeks to generate the best outcome (e.g., academic results and university entrance rankings) to become individually competitive in the employment market. The entrepreneurial subject is thus responsibilised within neoliberalism, promoting a hyper-realised form of meritocracy. If you are rich and successful, evidently it is because you deserve those riches and successes, and it has nothing to do with your social class or access to economic and cultural capital. However, if you are living in poverty or face significant disadvantage, this must be a result of your own choices and not due to the systemic structures that ensure that some people win and others must lose, despite the myth of meritocracy. Indeed, it is no secret that 'capitalism requires winners and losers, which makes for some uncomfortable tensions with an education system that seeks to uphold equity and democratic principles at its heart' (Riddle & Cleaver, 2017, p. 29).

Neoliberalism promotes greed and self-interest, creating entrepreneurs who compete and consume within the market. Despite the focus on the individual as the atomised and responsibilised subject, 'individuals have no intrinsic worth; their significance lies in their capacity to produce and consume ever more goods and services' (Fielding & Moss, 2010, p. 48). Competition is key to neoliberal ideology, which corresponds to a hyper-individualism and emphasis on performance, thus weakening important collective social bonds and commitment to the public good. Neoliberalism weakens the political substance of democracy, replacing it with *market democracy*—'once a term of derision for right-wing governance by unregulated capital—is now an ordinary descriptor for a form that has precisely nothing to do with the people ruling themselves' (Brown, 2011, p. 48). Further, Bauman (2004) argued that even the pursuit of happiness has become privatised and deregulated, subject to the machinations of the market, in which the public sphere is privatised and the public good gives way to individual interest. The atomisation of individuals and the removal of public life has taken its toll on a 'sense of common purpose and sapped our belief that, by working together, we can change life for the better. It has undermined democracy, and allowed intolerant and violent forces to fill the political vacuum. We are trapped in a vicious circle of alienation and reaction' (Monbiot, 2018, p. 24).

The logic of choice replaces meaningful public engagement within neoliberalised market economies, which can be observed through the tightly controlled electoral process in many contemporary capitalist liberal democracies. The choice between this candidate or that candidate, representatives of political parties with more in common than differences, ensures that the political class continues to produce policies that most directly benefit their corporate sponsors, rather than any idealised or actualised version of the public. Biesta (2014) contended that the marketisation of democracy to a reductive notion of choice has removed the possibility of transformative democratic engagement. Similarly, Brown (2011) argued that elections are more akin to circuses, in which the spectacle is key and carefully managed marketing campaigns seek to persuade voters to 'buy-in' to the message being sold to them. Democratic life shifts from a political act of engagement with the polis, to one of private consumption, whether at the hardware store or ballot box.

There has always been an uneasy tension between liberalism and democracy, which has been exacerbated through neoliberalism's focus on atomisation, marketisation and privatisation of what were formally public institutions and services. The ambivalent relationship between democracy and capitalism has long been understood, although the past few decades have seen a transformation of capitalism through neoliberalism, which has come to threaten the future of democracy (Ferrara, 2014). Instead of the public good, contemporary capitalism requires endless growth, increasing speed and consumption, along with inbuilt obsolescence as a driver of consumption (Taylor, 2019). Waste is not simply a by-product, but a necessary condition for capitalism to flourish (Bauman, 2017). As such, the production of endless surplus sits at the heart of the formation of the contemporary democratic subject, who becomes 'a being of excesses, an insatiable devourer of commodities, human rights and televisual spectacles, that the capitalist law of profit rules the planet' (Rancière, 2006, p. 88).

In addition, neoliberalism's triumph over social democracy has produced a form of compliant consumerist capitalism that supports and provides the political class and corporate oligarchs with the political and economic cover to act with impunity and in their own interests (Bloom & Sancino, 2019), with only superficial engagement with the notion of the public good, generally during key moments of the electoral cycle. Monbiot (2016) argued that powerful corporations and oligarchs are afforded special treatments, in the form of tax concessions, political favours, government contracts, relaxed media ownership laws, political donations and legal representation at all levels of power. To say that the one per cent are a powerful, oligarchic, global corporate elite is no understatement (Dorling, 2019). Under such conditions, Rancière (2006) argued that oligarchic elites permit the existence of democracy within defined and controllable limits, in which democratic passions are carefully redirected towards the pursuit of private pleasures rather than engagement in the public sphere. The public sphere becomes diminished from a place of shared deliberation to a platform on which the political class can appeal to private interests in the name of the collective good (Bauman, 2004).

Under neoliberalism, the apparatus of the social state is transformed to a mode of governance modelled on the corporation, which privatises public goods and turns them into private commodities. The rise of for-profit schools in many places around the globe is one example of the marketisation and privatisation of formerly public spaces. Another key area in which public infrastructure has been largely privatised is transport and energy. Public transport systems are now owned by private corporations, which are focused on returning profits to shareholders rather than the provision of a public service. Similarly, energy providers have been privatised and now operate in open, deregulated markets, competing for consumers rather than focusing on the delivery of an essential service. There are many examples of public goods that have been commodified and turned into private assets. The point is that these acts demonstrate how neoliberalism as an economic rationality has permeated across most walks of life, to become a catch-all political and social mode.

Schostak and Goodson (2020) argued that contemporary capitalism involves a clash between the utopian neoliberal ideal of the truly free individual, unfettered from society's limitations, to flourish within the market, and the concentration of wealth and economic power within a small globalised, corporate elite. As such, despite espousing the individual subject as the central player in neoliberalism, the sheer power of the oligarchs renders much of the tenets of liberal democracy redundant, 'displacing its basic principles of constitutionalism, legal equality, political and civil liberty, political autonomy, and universal inclusion with market criteria of cost/benefit ratios, efficiency, profitability, and efficacy' (Brown, 2011, p. 47). Neoliberalism models everything on the corporation, thus supressing democratic principles, instead asserting the supremacy of the entrepreneurial subject within the market. Under the conditions of neoliberal capitalism, democracy has transformed from a political concept to an economic one, in which a sense of collectivity and community responsibility has been 'largely replaced by individualistic notions of democracy as simply consumer choice' (Apple, 2004, p. 167). Rancière (2010) described contemporary democracy as a reign of narcissistic mass individualism, which has undermined collective forms of political agency and importantly, a sense of community. The possessive individualism of the consumer is 'inherently grounded in a process of deracing, declassing, and degendering' (Apple, 2006, p. 114), which decontextualises and decouples important issues of social and economic disadvantage from discussions of democracy, participation and equality.

Mouffe (2019) argued that the current context could be described as *post-democracy*, arising directly from the hegemonic status of neoliberalism and the central place of free market ideology across all levels of governance and policymaking. As a result, 'the agonistic tension between the liberal and the democratic principles, which is constitutive of liberal democracy, has been eliminated' (Mouffe, 2019, p. 16). This raises the question of whether a contemporary Western (or Western-styled) neoliberal capitalist society could be described as democratic, even in the thinnest version of the term. The arguments proposed by Mouffe (2019), Rancière (2006) and Giroux (2009) would suggest not, although this does not mean that we should abandon the project of re-democratising contemporary societies. Indeed, the current context of neoliberalised de-democratisation should see a doubling of re-democratisation efforts. Under neoliberalism, the state must be weakened enough so that it cannot effectively regulate against the excesses of predatory casino capitalism (Giroux, 2010). Instead, the *invisible hand* of the market must be free to be manipulated and mined for the highest profit margins possible by the corporate oligarchy. However, the state must not be weakened to the point where it can no longer hold back the will of the population—that is, the democratic impulses of the people (Rancière, 2006). A strong police force is necessary to contain and curtail democracy at home, combined with an imposing military machine that can ensure open trade routes and the continued flow of oil and other essential lubricants within the cogs of global capitalism. For example, the US has a $752.9 billion defence budget for 2022, which is in response to the 'pacing challenge from the People's Republic of China, combating the damaging effects of climate change on our military installations, and modernizing our capabilities to meet the advanced threats of tomorrow' (Department of Defense, 2021).

While the military and corporate sectors are supported through large funding allocations, legislation and other policy levers that enable an unencumbered realisation of neoliberal policy goals, the support for social policies that provide for social welfare, including income support and investment in public health and public education is eroded. Giroux (2009) argued that this is a deliberate effect of contemporary governments that purport to be democratic and inclusive—such as the US, UK and Australia—while excluding and othering young people from marginalised and disenfranchised backgrounds from meaningful access to schooling, work and civic participation. Young people become waste (Bauman, 2017) because they are surplus to the needs of the elite. Indeed, radically democratic cooperation in social welfare through health, education and childcare is perceived as being a direct threat to neoliberal capitalism (Amsler, 2015).

Much of Apple's work (e.g., Apple, 2004, 2006, 2013, 2014) has focused on the alliance between neoliberal and neoconservative interests in education, through its effects on school policy and curriculum. While neoliberalism seeks to commodify education and turn schooling into a market, neoconservatism seeks to revert the social order back to an assumed vision of the gendered, raced and classed order of yesteryear. Apple (2013) claimed that while neoliberalism seeks a weakened state, neoconservatism demands a strengthened state in areas of social policymaking, 'especially over the politics of the body and gender and race relations, over standards, values, and conduct, and over what knowledge should be passed on to future generations' (p. 200). Thus, curriculum is deeply enmeshed in the ongoing process of neoconservative and neoliberal refashioning of education, in which schools are remade to serve the purpose of producing entrepreneurial responsibilised workers, who are also compliant and docile subjects of the neoconservative society. There are serious implications for access and engagement with meaningful forms of schooling because within the context of neoliberal education policymaking has been for governments and education policymakers 'to double down on reductive and technicist modes of school governance, curriculum, and pedagogy, giving rise to further intrusions on the professional autonomy of teachers and the rights of young people to demand access to socially inclusive and supportive education opportunities' (Riddle, 2019, p. 3).

Further, neoconservatism works to maintain social hierarchies that benefit the elite, including the political class and corporate oligarchs, which can be observed in the growth of demand for high-fee independent schooling in Australia. The stratified schooling system in Australia has made it one of the most unequal in the OECD, with vast differences between the resourcing and funding available to independent schools that service the rich, compared with the residualisation that occurs with the poorest public schools, which service some of the most disadvantaged and impoverished communities in the country. However, this is all good and proper within a neoliberal worldview because it comes down to a question of merit and choice. The accumulation of wealth is seen to be 'proof of being naturally talented, hard-working risk takers' (Schostak & Goodson, 2020, p. 38), rather than being in a position of considerable advantage due to the structural inequality built into the social and economic systems of society.

Bloom and Sancino (2019) argued that the decaying of democratic culture under neoliberalism has led to a dramatic deskilling of the population. Further, they claimed that the political and public spheres have been hollowed out, 'in which an ever-narrower set of ideological choices and policies was fought over with an ever-higher degree of passionate partisanship' (Bloom & Sancino, 2019, p. 25). Technocrats and marketing managers are the new driving force between the policymaking and electioneering of the political class, running the numbers via polls and focus groups to determine the effects of this strategy or that process. In the meantime, democracy is reduced to a bump in opinion polls or the consumer-driven feedback of the corporation. Extending this argument, Schostak and Goodson (2020) claimed that these forces act within a pseudo-democracy, in which the management of opinion is the key to ensuring that the elite retain their position by subverting 'education' and 'research' to their own ends. However, these false neoliberal narratives have their limitations because:

> Humans are incapable of functioning and living together without a good story to bind them and keep a certain set of values intact. That's why the

lack of a story in neoliberalism, the lack of meaning and cause, can be unbearable for the human mind. Since humans are forced to live in a state of mild antipathy—an acceptable amount of antipathy that is crucial to the neoliberal system—they are forever in dire need of a cause, a central triangulation point that they can use to orientate themselves in relation to what's good and what's bad. The ethical vacuum of neoliberalism, its dismissal of the fact that human nature needs meaning and desperately seeks reasons to live, creates fertile ground for the invention of causes, and sometimes the most groundless or shallowest ones. Contrary to what those who defend the system believe, the desire to have more, or the fear of having less, can never fill the void in a human mind.

(Temelkuran, 2019, p. 113)

Neoliberalism has perhaps reached its limit, as we are rapidly coming to realise during the midst of a global pandemic and climate catastrophe, during which our political and corporate 'leaders' have manifestly failed to respond adequately to the challenges posed by multiple crises, and through which the capitalist machine has continued to churn out winners and losers at an ever-increasing pace. Mouffe (2019) contended that 'we are witnessing a crisis of the neoliberal hegemonic formation and this crisis opens the possibility for the construction of a more democratic order' (p. 1). Perhaps our contemporary forms of democracy—realised through the thin versions afforded by neoliberalism, neoconservatism and capitalism—have completely failed us, in which case, 'only an alternative vision can bring about universal prosperity and emancipation. Articulating and achieving this better world is the fundamental task of the left today' (Srnicek & Williams, 2016, p. 3). The question remains, what would a democracy that is worthy of its name in the twenty-first century look like, and what role does education and schooling have in its formation, articulation and realisation?

The Possibility of a New Democratic Horizon

It seems clear that we are at an important threshold, in which the coming decades will come to demonstrate whether twenty-first century democracy is up to the challenge of responding to the multiple crises facing societies around the world. Neoliberalism and its manifestations of predatory globalised capitalism—married to a regressive neoconservative politics that produces new forms of racist, sexist, classist, ableist ideologies, and in some cases more virulent and extreme forms of populism, demagoguery and neofascism—cannot be tolerated as a way forward. As Carr (2011) argued, 'the problem is not that democracy is not a worthy concept but, rather, that the type of democracy that has received normative, relativistic salience is, in many regards, anti-democratic' (Carr, 2011, p. 4). We need something else to act as a new democratic horizon, which opens up new possibilities for a more sustainable and inclusive future, within which education is key. Democracy is in crisis, but we have not yet reached the end of the democratic dream. Mouffe (1993) claimed that:

> Far from being the necessary result of a moral evolution of humankind, democracy is something uncertain and improbable and must never be taken for granted. It is an always fragile conquest that needs to be defended as well as deepened. There is no threshold of democracy that once reached will guarantee its continued existence. Democracy is in peril not only when there is insufficient consensus and allegiance to the values it embodies, but also when its agonistic dynamic is hindered by an apparent excess of consensus, which usually masks a disquieting apathy. It is also endangered by the growing marginalization of entire groups whose status as an 'underclass' practically puts them outside the political community.
>
> *(p. 6)*

The version of neoliberal market democracy encouraged by the elites is an exclusionary force, which perpetuates social inequality and ensures that marginalised groups cannot meaningfully participate in public life. Rancière (2010) described this as a bourgeois democracy, which works to conceal the realities of exploitation and inequality that sit at its heart, alongside the erosion of the public good. Indeed, the very notion of the public is commodified and sold back to consumers within the marketplace. Health and education are two key arenas in which the public-made-private manifest in unequal access and opportunities, with large swathes of young people left out. Any democracy worth of the name needs to radically reconfigure the economic, political and social relationships to ensure a more robust and inclusive set of practices, institutions and discourses that support the participation of all people in democracy. Further, Amsler (2015) claimed that people living in 'extreme neoliberal societies' such as the US, UK and Australia—'those where the politico–economic, cultural and cognitive hegemony of neoliberal capitalism penetrate the fibres of everyday life, social relationships and institutional organization—are once again looking for these resources of hope and straining in the directions from which they reckon they might come' (p. 3).

However, tinkering around the edges of democracy will not suffice, if the superstructures of capitalism and neoliberalism are left untouched because 'the reality of complex, globalised capitalism is that small interventions consisting of relatively non-scalable actions are highly unlikely to ever be able to reorganise our socioeconomic system' (Srnicek & Williams, 2016, p. 29). We need to conceive of radical change, and then be steadfast in the will to reconfigure society to be more sustainable, inclusive and just, both between people and with the animals, lands and waterways upon which we depend for our continued survival on this finite planet. Bauman (2004) explained that people cannot simply 'stop imagining things as different from what they are now. We can't just settle for what "is" because we cannot grasp what "is" without reaching beyond it'

(p. 64). What is needed is the creation of a new public ethics (Schostak & Goodson, 2020), which is premised on the promise of radical equality and inclusion.

Bloom and Sancino (2019) suggested that the rapid integration of smart technologies—artificial intelligence, automation, social media, robotics and ubiquitous spread of algorithmic decision-making—presents both a threat and an opportunity for twenty-first century democracy. Technological advances can open new possibilities for combating some of the gravest challenges facing societies, such as the development of vaccines for the COVID-19 pandemic, new technologies for carbon capture and climate change mitigation, plus other advances in health, agriculture and sustainable development. However, technologies can also widen existing social and economic inequalities, creating new social division and upheaval that results in widespread harm. For example, the ubiquity of social media has enabled fast transmission of information between large groups of people, yet has also fostered growing distrust in scientific evidence and truth, resulting in the emergence of forms of 'alternative facts' and 'post-truth' epistemologies. The effects of these are only beginning to be clearly understood, and Chapter 3 spends some time unpacking the crisis of truth and trust in an age of pandemics and populism.

Although democracy is a moral idea that can never be fully realised in practice (Carr & Hartnett, 1996), it is possible to continue to expand the possibilities for meaningful engagement and participation in democratic modes of being and becoming, in which public institutions and civic life are available to all people. Fielding and Moss (2010) claimed that democracy should be taken as the starting point 'because it holds an important key to how we, as societies and a species, may (if we are lucky) be able to defuse the dangers facing us and take a new direction that is better able to assure survival and flourishing' (p. 57). There is hope to be found in democracy, which Amsler (2015) described as being achievable through radical social resistance and transformation, and perhaps most importantly, through the political work of education to shape a commitment to civic participation and collective activity.

Giroux (2016) argued that democracy is in retreat and that neoconservatives in places such as the US have gained the upper hand in claiming a spiritual–moral crisis in wider culture, which has resulted in a moral crisis in schooling. The answer is to increase authoritarian policies and structures within schooling to ensure greater obedience, but importantly, not for all young people. Those who attend the schools that cater for the wealthy elite shall continue to receive a classically liberal education, steeped in literature, arts, history and critical–cultural perspectives. However, those young people whose first mistake was to be born poor or into marginalised communities shall receive an impoverished schooling that is measured by metrics on standardised testing and subjected to careful monitoring and control to ensure that they are learning how to be compliant consumers and a cheap future labour force. The emphasis on job readiness removes questions about how young people become informed, critical and creative citizens who can participate meaningfully in public life (Aronowitz,

2008). This must change if we are to reimagine democracy and education in more inclusive and sustainable ways, in which young people regardless of their backgrounds and life experiences are afforded the opportunity to meaningfully engage in society as equals.

As one possible act of reimagining liberal–democratic societies, Dorling (2019) has called for a slow revolution, one which reclaims democracy from the corporate oligarchy and the one per cent to ensure a more fully realised and thicker version of democracy that includes everyone, especially marginalised groups who have been traditionally disenfranchised. Conversely, Taylor (2019) has argued that a reimagined democratic social contract requires the deliberate withdrawal of consent and a 'coordinated campaign of constructive coercion' in the name of restorative justice (p. 161); that is, a massive civil disobedience movement is called for on the part of the populace against the corporate elites and political class, which seeks to maintain its own power and privilege. However, as Mouffe (2019) warned, the 'extension and radicalization of democratic struggles would never achieve a fully liberated society and the emancipatory project could not be conceived any longer as the elimination of the State. There will always be antagonisms, struggles and partial opaqueness of the social' (p. 1). Nevertheless, the people must persist to forge a more inclusive and caring democracy, one which is able to intervene and adequately respond to the challenges of the twenty-first century.

To where should we look for the possibilities from a new democratic horizon? Perhaps Rancière (2006, 2010) and Mouffe (1993, 2019) offer some productive ways to consider the question. Their formulations of an agonistic democracy predicated on the radical equality between individuals who engage in dissensus—the productive act of disagreement—provide opportunities to consider a more fully democratic future. As one example, Mouffe (2019) suggested the creation of a *left populism* to intervene in the current crisis of hegemonic democracy, which works in the interest of powerful elites, while excluding and marginalising many others. She argued that 'it is necessary to establish a political frontier and that left populism, understood as a discursive strategy of construction of the political frontier between "the people" and "the oligarchy", constitutes, in the present conjuncture, the type of politics needed to recover and deepen democracy' (Mouffe, 2019, p. 5). Importantly, democracy is not the power of the poor, the people, the masses, but rather the power of those who, Rancière (2010) explained, have no qualification for the exercising of power. While consensus is important in some contexts, likewise the possibility of choice between real alternatives offered by agonistic pluralism presents the condition of existence of democracy in practice (Mouffe, 1993).

Additionally, Waldron (2010) called for a more agonistic politics, which seeks to be seen and heard, while paying attention to the other. This requires openness, 'toleration, patience, and the ability to reflect and reconsider. No one is above the debate and no one's contributions are beneath the attention of others' (Waldron, 2010, p. 32). Agonistic pluralism 'presupposes that the "other" is no longer seen as an enemy to be destroyed, but as an "adversary", i.e., somebody with whose ideas we are going to struggle but whose right to defend those ideas we will not put into question' (Mouffe, 1999, p. 755). In support of this position, Schostak (2019) claimed that radical democracy requires the promotion and equality of different voices across all sectors of life and social interaction to ensure that democratic societies do not give way to fascism and other forms of authoritarianism. A more fully engaged public can help to ensure that democracy moves away from its normative, hegemonic state of thin representative democracy, to one that is a more 'transformative, critically engaged, *thicker* democracy' (Carr & Thésée, 2019, p. 80).

A more fully realised, thicker democracy can be nurtured through a more democratic mode of education, in which the participation and engagement of young people is central to the meaning-making, social learning and curriculum experiences that take place within the schoolyard. As Fielding and Moss (2010) explained, we do not have to settle for the current version of neoliberalised schooling policy, in which schools are quasi-businesses selling education products to consumers (i.e., parents and students) in a marketplace, but can instead seek a more democratic system of education 'that treats schools as public institutions and parents and children as citizens, capable of engaging in a democratic way of life and democratic forms of relationship, including participation in the making of collective choices' (p. 60). Importantly, all children would benefit from a more critical, democratic, caring approach to schooling that is presupposed on the assumptions of thick democracy, participation and equality.

While civics education works as an important bulwark against fascism and authoritarianism (Mounk, 2018), there needs to be a shift from teaching citizenship to learning through democracy, which enables young people to enact democratic participation and to engage in civic discourses as members of society who are already in relationship with each other and the broader communities within which they reside (Biesta, 2011). This is a critical feature of the notion of a schooling that is for democracy, rather than schooling about democracy, which has been the purview of traditional approaches to civics and citizenship curriculum. As Apple (2004) maintained:

> As long as the struggle for a socially just and critically democratic education continues, there will be no end in sight. But that's the point isn't it? Education is an inherently political and ethical—and fully human—act. There is no way of eliding our responsibilities here. These issues will not go away and new generations will need to continue our understanding of and action on relations of dominance and inequality.
>
> *(p. 174)*

This chapter has provided a brief appraisal of the contemporary state of democracy in the first decades of the twenty-first century, outlining some of the key challenges facing societies that call themselves liberal democracies. The point is not to claim that the democratic dream is over, but rather to reclaim a more fully realised, thicker version of democracy that is based on agonism, pluralism and dissensus as its modes of practice and encounter. Education is at the heart of any project to reconceive democracy, so must the formal sites of education—early childhood education and care, primary and secondary schools, universities, technical colleges and other adult learning institutions—be part of any conversation about how society sees its citizens and their engagement with the public discourses, institutions and challenges. In a time of unprecedented crisis, the need is more urgent than ever before, to consider the ways in which democracy and education can help young people to tackle the existential threats that they will face in the coming years. It is not enough to continue with schooling as usual in the face of rapid destabilisation, growing inequality and increasing risk. We need a new democratic horizon that opens up new possibilities for living and learning together.

References

Amnesty International. (2020, 13 August). Belarus: Mounting evidence of a campaign of widespread torture of peaceful protesters. *Amnesty International.* https://www.amnesty.org/en/latest/news/2020/08/belarus-mounting-evidence-of-a-campaign-of-widespread-torture-of-peaceful-protesters/

Amsler, S. S. (2015). *The education of radical democracy.* Routledge.

Apple, M. W. (2004). *Ideology and curriculum* (2nd ed.). RoutledgeFalmer.

Apple, M. W. (2006). *Educating the 'right' way: Markets, standards, God and inequality* (2nd ed.). Routledge.

Apple, M. W. (2013). *Knowledge, power and education.* Routledge.

Apple, M. W. (2014). *Official knowledge: Democratic education in a conservative age* (3rd ed.). Routledge.

Apple, M. W., & Beane, J. A. (Eds.). (2007). *Democratic schools: Lessons in powerful education* (2nd ed.). Heinemann.

Arendt, H. (1969). *Between past and future: Eight exercises in political thought.* The Viking Press.

Aronowitz, S. (2008). *Against schooling: Toward an education that matters.* Paradigm Publishers.

Aslam, A. (2017). *Ordinary democracy: Sovereignty and citizenship beyond the neoliberal impasse.* Oxford University Press.

Bauman, Z. (2004). To hope is human. *Tikkun, 19*(6), 64–67.

Bauman, Z. (2017). *Wasted lives: Modernity and its outcasts.* Polity Press.

BBC News. (2020, 23 January). Myanmar Rohingya: What you need to know about the crisis. *BBC News.* https://www.bbc.com/news/world-asia-41566561

Beane, J. A., & Apple, M. W. (2007). The case for democratic schools. In M. W. Apple & J. A. Beane (Eds.), *Democratic schools: Lessons in powerful education* (2nd ed., pp. 1–29). Heinemann.

Bensaïd, D. (2011). Permanent scandal. In G. Agamben, A. Badiou, D. Bensaïd, W. Brown, J.-L. Nancy, J. Rancière, K. Ross, & S. Žižek (Eds.), *Democracy in what state?* (pp. 16–43). Columbia University Press.

Berti, B. (2015). The Syrian refugee crisis: Regional and human security implications. *Strategic Assessment, 17*(4), 41–53.

Biesta, G. (2011). *Learning democracy in school and society: Education, lifelong learning, and the politics of citizenship.* Sense Publishers.

Biesta, G. (2014). Learning in public places: Civic learning for the twenty-first century. In G. Biesta, M. De Bie, & Wildemeersch (Eds.), *Civic learning, democratic citizenship and the public sphere* (pp. 1–11). Springer.

Bloom, P., & Sancino, A. (2019). *Disruptive democracy: The clash between techno-populism and techno-democracy.* Sage.

Boot, M. (2021, 4 August). Yes, Trump tried to stage a coup. By denying it, the right is laying the groundwork for another one. *The Washington Post.* https://www.washingtonpost.com/opinions/2021/08/04/republican-denial-capitol-insurrection-preparing-way-for-future-dangers/

Brown, W. (2011). 'We are all democrats now…'. In G. Agamben, A. Badiou, D. Bensaïd, W. Brown, J.-L. Nancy, J. Rancière, K. Ross, & S. Žižek (Eds.), *Democracy in what state?* (pp. 44–57). Columbia University Press.

Bump, P. (2021, 12 July). Donald Trump has completed his journey toward embracing the Capitol rioters. *The Washington Post.* https://www.washingtonpost.com/politics/2021/07/12/donald-trump-has-completed-his-journey-toward-embracing-capitol-rioters/

Carey, A. (1995). *Taking the risk out of democracy: Corporate propaganda in the US and Australia.* University of New South Wales Press.

Carr, P. R. (2008). Educators and education for democracy: Moving beyond 'thin' democracy. *Interamerican Journal of Education for Democracy, 1*(2), 147–165.

Carr, P. R. (2010). Re-thinking normative democracy and the political economy of education. *Journal for Critical Education Policy Studies, 8*(1), 1–40.

Carr, P. R. (2011). *Does your vote count? Critical pedagogy and democracy.* Peter Lang.

Carr, P. R., & Thésée, G. (2019). *It's not education that scares me, it's the educators: Is there still hope for democracy in education, and education for democracy?* Myers Education Press.

Carr, W., & Hartnett, A. (1996). *Education and the struggle for democracy: The politics of educational ideas.* Open University Press.

Cathey, L., & Keneally, M. (2020, 30 May). A look back at Trump comments perceived by some as inciting violence. *ABC News.* https://abcnews.go.com/Politics/back-trump-comments-perceived-encouraging-violence/story?id=48415766

Conley, H. A., & Green, M. J. (2021, 22 September). Don't underestimate the AUKUS rift with France. *Foreign Policy.* https://foreignpolicy.com/2021/09/22/aukus-france-biden-europe-allies/

Counts, G. S. (1932). *Dare the school build a new social order?* The John Day Company.

Cox, D. A. (2021, 11 February). After the ballots are counted: Conspiracies, political violence and American exceptionalism. Findings from the January 2021 American Perspectives Survey. *Survey Center on American Life.* https://www.americansurveycenter.org/research/after-the-ballots-are-counted-conspiracies-political-violence-and-american-exceptionalism/

Dallmayr, F. (2017). *Democracy to come: Politics as relational praxis.* Oxford University Press.

Department of Defense. (2021, 28 May). *The Department of Defense releases the president's fiscal year 2022 defense budget.* https://www.defense.gov/Newsroom/Releases/Release/Article/2638711/the-department-of-defense-releases-the-presidents-fiscal-year-2022-defense-budg/

Dewey, J. (1916). *Democracy and education: An introduction to the philosophy of education.* The Macmillan Company.

Dorling, D. (2019). *Inequality and the 1%.* Verso.

Ferrara, A. (2014). *The democratic horizon: Hyperpluralism and the renewal of political liberalism.* Cambridge University Press.

Fielding, M., & Moss, P. (2010). *Radical education and the common school: A democratic alternative.* Routledge.

Frega, R. (2019). *Pragmatism and the wide view of democracy.* Palgrave Macmillan.

Garton Ash, T. (2020, 9 December). The future of liberalism. *Prospect Magazine*. https://www.prospectmagazine.co.uk/magazine/the-future-of-liberalism-brexit-trump-philosophy

Giroux, H. A. (2009). *Youth in a suspect society: Democracy or disposability?* Palgrave Macmillan.

Giroux, H. A. (2010). *Zombie politics and culture in the age of casino capitalism*. Peter Lang.

Giroux, H. A. (2016). *Schooling and the struggle for public life: Democracy's promise and education's challenge* (2nd ed.). Routledge.

Goodlad, J. I. (1997). Reprise and a look ahead. In J. I. Goodlad & T. J. McMannon (Eds.), *The public purpose of education and schooling* (pp. 155–167). Jossey-Bass Publishers.

Hoekstra, A. (2019, 30 May). Myanmar's democracy is letting down a young generation. *Deutsche Welle*. https://www.dw.com/en/myanmars-democracy-is-letting-down-a-young-generation/a-48976172

Hubbard, B. (2020, 8 April). Syria used chemical weapons 3 times in one week, watchdog says. *The New York Times*. https://www.nytimes.com/2020/04/08/world/middleeast/syria-assad-chemical-weapons.html

Human Rights Watch. (2021, 13 January). Belarus: Unprecedented crackdown. *Human Rights Watch*. https://www.hrw.org/news/2021/01/13/belarus-unprecedented-crackdown

Ilyushina, M. (2021, 27 May). Belarus leader claims plane diversion protected passengers, says country is under 'hybrid attack'. *The Washington Post*. https://www.washingtonpost.com/world/2021/05/26/belarus-plane-lukashenko-protasevich/

International Court of Justice. (2020, 23 January). *Application of the Convention on the Prevention and Punishment of the Crime of Genocide (The Gambia v. Myanmar)*. Order of 23 January 2020: Request for the indication of provisional measures. https://www.icj-cij.org/public/files/case-related/178/178-20200123-ORD-01-00-EN.pdf

Loopstra, R., Reeves, A., & Tarasuk, V. (2019). The rise of hunger among low-income households: An analysis of the risks of food insecurity between 2004 and 2016 in a population-based study of UK adults. *Journal of Epidemiology and Community Health*, 73(7), 668–673. https://doi.org/10.1136/jech-2018-211194

Makhovsky, A. (2020, 25 August). Belarus jails two opposition leaders; teachers head rally of thousands. *Reuters*. https://www.reuters.com/article/us-belarus-election-idUSKBN25L19Z

Markell, P. (2010). The rule of the people: Arendt, *arché*, and democracy. In S. Benhabib (Ed.), *Politics in dark times: Encounters with Hannah Arendt* (pp. 58–82). Cambridge University Press.

McChesney, R. (1999). *Profit over people: Neoliberalism and the global order*. Seven Stories Press.

McLaren, P., & Farahmandpur, R. (2005). *Teaching against global capitalism and the new imperialism: A critical pedagogy*. Rowman & Littlefield Publishers.

Monbiot, G. (2016). *How did we get into this mess? Politics, equality, nature*. Verso.

Monbiot, G. (2018). *Out of the wreckage: A new politics for an age of crisis*. Verso.

Monbiot, G. (2020, 11 November). The US was lucky to get Trump: Biden may pave the way for a more competent autocrat. *The Guardian*. https://www.theguardian.com/commentisfree/2020/nov/11/us-trump-biden-president-elect

Mouffe, C. (1993). *The return of the political*. Verso.

Mouffe, C. (1999). Deliberative democracy or agonistic pluralism? *Social Research*, 66(3), 745–758.

Mouffe, C. (2019). *For a left populism*. Verso.

Mounk, T. (2018). *The people vs. democracy: Why our freedom is in danger and how to save it*. Harvard University Press.

Mun, K. (2021, 15 January). Democracy in Myanmar still under threat. *East Asia Forum*. https://www.eastasiaforum.org/2021/01/15/democracy-in-myanmar-still-under-threat/

Nepogodin, A. (2020, 21 November). 'We don't need such a future': Belarusian students and teachers about youth protests, persecution and migration. *Voice of Belarus*. https://www.voiceofbelarus.com/we-dont-need-such-a-future/

Nilsen, M. (2013). Will democracy bring peace to Myanmar? *International Area Studies Review*, *16*(2), 115–141. https://doi.org/10.1177/2233865913492961

Rancière, J. (2006). *Hatred of democracy*. Verso.

Rancière, J. (2010). *Dissensus: On politics and aesthetics*. Continuum.

Ratcliffe, R. (2021, 28 July). Myanmar could become COVID 'super-spreader' state, says UN expert. *The Guardian*. https://www.theguardian.com/world/2021/jul/28/myanmar-could-become-covid-super-spreader-state-says-un-expert

Renshaw, C. (2021, 25 February). Myanmar on trial: Is the country's military on the run from international law? *Asia & the Pacific Policy Society: Policy Forum*. https://www.policyforum.net/myanmar-on-trial/

Reuters. (2021a, 23 May). More than 125,000 Myanmar teachers suspended for opposing coup. *Reuters*. https://www.reuters.com/world/asia-pacific/more-than-125000-myanmar-teachers-suspended-opposing-coup-2021-05-23/

Reuters. (2021b, 28 May). Syria's Assad wins 4th term with 95% of vote, in election the West calls fraudulent. *Reuters*. https://www.reuters.com/world/middle-east/syrias-president-bashar-al-assad-wins-fourth-term-office-with-951-votes-live-2021-05-27/

Riddle, S. (2019). Democracy and education in local–global contexts. *The International Education Journal: Comparative Perspectives*, *18*(1), 1–6.

Riddle, S., & Apple, M. W. (2019). Education and democracy in dangerous times. In S. Riddle & M. W. Apple (Eds.), *Re-imagining education for democracy* (pp. 1–9). Routledge.

Riddle, S., & Cleaver, D. (2017). *Alternative schooling, social justice and marginalised students*. Palgrave Macmillan.

Riddle, S., & Heffernan, A. (2018). Education and democracy for complex contemporary childhoods. *Global Studies of Childhood*, *8*(4), 319–324. https://doi.org/10.1177/2043610618817370

Roth, A., & Auseyushkin, Y. (2020, 11 August). Belarus opposition candidate rejects election result after night of protests. *The Guardian*. https://www.theguardian.com/world/2020/aug/10/belarus-opposition-candidate-rejects-election-result-protests-svetlana-tikhanovskaya-lukashenko

Schostak, J. (2019). 'Towards a society of equals': Democracy, education, cooperation and the practice of radical inclusion. *International Journal of Inclusive Education*, *23*(11), 1103–1115. https://doi.org/10.1080/13603116.2019.1629161

Schostak, J., & Goodson, I. (2020). *Democracy, education and research: The struggle for public life*. Routledge.

Smith, H. (1995). It's education for, not about, democracy. *Educational Horizons*, *73*(2), 62–69.

Srnicek, N., & Williams, A. (2016). *Inventing the future: Postcapitalism and a world without work*. Verso.

Stoke, K., & Aung, S. M. (2020). Transition to democracy or hybrid regime? The dynamics and outcomes of democratization in Myanmar. *The European Journal of Development Research*, *32*, 274–293. https://doi.org/10.1057/s41287-019-00247-x

Street, P. (2015). *They rule: The 1% vs. democracy*. Routledge.

Swift, R. (2002). *The nonsense guide to democracy*. New International Publications.

Taylor, A. (2019). *Democracy may not exist, but we'll miss it when it's gone*. Verso.

Temelkuran, E. (2019). *How to lose a country: The seven steps from democracy to dictatorship*. 4th Estate.

Tufekci, Z. (2020, 7 November). America's next authoritarian will be much more competent. *The Atlantic*. https://www.theatlantic.com/ideas/archive/2020/11/trump-proved-authoritarians-can-get-elected-america/617023/

Waldron, J. (2010). Arendt on the foundations of equality. In S. Benhabib (Ed.), *Politics in dark times: Encounters with Hannah Arendt* (pp. 17–39). Cambridge University Press.

Wild, W., LeBlanc, P., & Rose, R. (2021, 3 August). 2 more DC police officers who responded to Capitol insurrection have died by suicide. *CNN*. https://edition.cnn.com/2021/08/02/politics/dc-metropolitan-police-officer-suicide-january-6-capitol-riot/index.html

Zakaria, F. (1997). The rise of illiberal democracy. *Foreign Affairs*, 76, 22–43.

Ziady, H. (2021, 25 May). Airlines avoid Belarus after 'state-sponsored hijacking' of Ryanair flight. *CNN*. https://edition.cnn.com/2021/05/24/business/airlines-belarus-air-space/index.html

Zuboff, S. (2019). *The age of surveillance capitalism: The fight for a human future at the new frontier of power*. Public Affairs.

3
PANDEMICS AND POPULISM IN A POST-TRUTH WORLD

Introduction

> It is the epidemic of fear, not only of COVID-19, that has descended upon the world.
>
> (Lévy, 2020, p. viii)

The Severe Acute Respiratory Syndrome Coronavirus 2 (SARS-CoV-2) and its accompanying disease, the 2019 Novel Coronavirus (COVID-19) swept the globe during 2020 and 2021. To say that the world has irrevocably changed in the wake of the COVID-19 global pandemic is no exaggeration. For example, Giroux (2020) argued that the pandemic presents a medical, political and ideological crisis, which is deeply rooted in decades of neoliberal policies and widespread social and economic inequalities. Further, the pandemic has laid bare the crises of liberal democracy and capitalism, as well as exposing the harm being wrought on the ecosystems that sustain life on the planet. Clearly, there cannot be a return to the way that things were, although there is no guarantee that we will find a path that leads us to a more inclusive, caring and sustaining society. Too much hangs in the balance and too much remains unknown to say with any certainty where we will go, but there is no doubt that a commitment to reimagining more democratic modes of governance should be central to the project of building a future worthy of the name. Schwab and Malleret (2020) claimed that:

> The worldwide crisis triggered by the coronavirus pandemic has no parallel in modern history. We cannot be accused of hyperbole when we say it is plunging our world in its entirety and each of us individually into the most challenging times we've faced in generations. It is our defining

moment—we will be dealing with its fallout for years, and many things will change forever. It is bringing economic disruption of monumental proportions, creating a dangerous and volatile period on multiple fronts—politically, socially, geopolitically—raising deep concerns about the environment and also extending the reach (pernicious or otherwise) of technology into our lives.

(p. 11)

While the emergence of COVID-19 in early 2020 marks a significant turning point in human experience, one could easily draw back the timeline and suggest, following Lévy (2020), that the epidemic of fear is the greater threat, and it is one that has been building for much longer. Similarly, Degerman et al. (2020) argued that the defining feature of the multiple crises facing contemporary society is fear. Although there are multiple points of entry, for the analyses presented in this chapter, the point of entry will be the election of Donald Trump to the US presidency in 2016, which heralded calls of the death of truth through the rise of 'fake news' and alternative facts. However, even Trump's ascendancy relied on much deeper, long-term erosions of trust in public institutions. The rise of anti-democratic forces in populist politics preceded Trump, and they have also outlived his tenure. This chapter seeks to position the COVID-19 global pandemic, Trumpism and the death of truth and trust through the resurgence of populist politics and rising anti-democratic sentiment, within the broader contours of human experience in the first decades of the twenty-first century. By understanding the multiple intersecting crises of truth, trust and fear during a time of rapid social, political and economic upheaval, perhaps we can come to better understand a way forward that is more democratic and able to respond to the great challenges ahead.

Writing on the sociology of COVID-19, Connell (2020) observed that a striking feature of the pandemic has been its coming at a time when many of the world's supposedly free, liberal democracies are 'controlled by narrow-minded neo-conservative governments, closely aligned with corporate elites, trading on nationalism, racist fearmongering and religious antagonisms to sustain their popular support' (p. 748). The erosion of trust in public institutions and the challenge to social cohesion, caused by widening inequality, fear and ignorance, provided a welcoming set of circumstances for a microscopic not-quite-alive infection machine to attach itself with ease to the global body, causing irreparable harm in the process and changing the ways in which we live our everyday lives, now and into the future. This chapter considers how pandemics and populism have come to act as a 'new normal' for contemporary societies as democratic systems and institutions appear unable to effectively cope with the serious challenges facing them. A more democratic mode of schooling is proposed as one potential response to the destabilising effects of alternative facts, Trumpism and the erosion of trust in expertise during the middle of a global public health crisis.

Pandemic as Neither Beginning Nor End

> We are caught in a triple crisis: medical (the epidemic itself), economic (which will hit hard whatever the outcome of the epidemic), and psychological. The basic coordinates of the everyday lives of millions are disintegrating, and the change will affect everything, from flying to holidays to simple bodily contact.
>
> *(Žižek, 2020, p. 90)*

When reports first began to emerge in December 2019 that there was a novel coronavirus circulating in the Chinese province of Wuhan, it seemed like a distant problem here in Australia, given we were in the midst of a catastrophic climate change-fuelled wildfire season on the east coast, and a prime minister who had secretly escaped to holiday in Hawaii (Albeck-Ripka et al., 2020). By September 2021, more than 230 million cases and 4.7 million deaths had been officially recorded, although many experts suggest that in many places such as India and Brazil, the case and death figures could be significantly underreported (Dong et al., 2020; Pradhan & Chaudhary, 2021). Tracking excess deaths over the duration of the pandemic can provide a more comprehensive indication of the broader impact of the pandemic because 'it captures not only the confirmed deaths, but also COVID-19 deaths that were not correctly diagnosed and reported as well as deaths from other causes that are attributable to the overall crisis conditions' (Giattino et al., 2021, np). Some estimates place the current global COVID-19 toll at more than three times the official count (Institute for Health Metrics and Evaluation, 2021).

Of course, the death toll is not the only measure of the catastrophic impacts of COVID-19. The emergence of 'long COVID' is only just beginning to be understood, which presents as a range of debilitating and chronic health effects and is a cause of significant concern (Davis et al., 2021). Further, substantial evidence is emerging of the effects of widespread lockdowns and restrictions and their toll on physical and mental health and well-being (e.g., Cullen et al., 2020; Prati & Mancini, 2021; Vindegaard & Benros, 2020). Giroux (2020) was particularly salient in his analysis:

> The coronavirus pandemic has pulled back the curtain to reveal the power of a brutal neoliberalism—and its global financial markets—in all of its cruelty. This is a system that has not only eroded the democratic ideals of equality and popular sovereignty, but has also created a political and economic context in which the looming pandemic puts a severe strain on medical workers and hospitals that lack ventilators and other essential equipment to treat patients and limit the number of deaths caused by the virus. This points to a moment in the current historical conjuncture in which the space between the passing of one period and the beginning of a

new age offers the possibility for the social and political imagination to set in motion a global movement for radical democracy.

(np)

Speaking on the BBC's *The Inquiry* program in 2014, Larry Brilliant, a key figure in the global campaign to eradicate smallpox, claimed that 'outbreaks are inevitable; pandemics are optional' (BBC, 2014). The warnings were clear: SARS, MERS, swine flu, avian flu and Ebola all punctuated the first two decades of the twenty-first century. Based on the premise of a deadly global pandemic, 2011 film *Contagion* now seems like a prescient warning rather than a work of fiction. Indeed, the film enjoyed a resurgence of popularity on streaming services during the long lockdowns of 2020. Microsoft founder and billionaire Bill Gates claimed, in a 2015 TED talk, that 'if anything kills over 10 million people in the next few decades, it's most likely to be a highly infectious virus rather than a war. Not missiles, but microbes. … But we've actually invested very little in a system to stop an epidemic. We're not ready' (Gates, 2015, np). It turned out that these comments precisely discerned our current predicament.

Of course, hindsight is a rather pointless skill that most people seem to possess in abundance, although clearly there were many opportunities for governments to employ some foresight prior to the onset of the pandemic. In the main, liberal–democratic governments the world over were slow to respond to the threat of COVID-19, and then once the threat was fully realised, the move from open movement to police-enforced 'stay at home' orders quickly swept the globe. Perhaps nowhere was more obviously brutal in the curtailing of civil liberties than in the original Wuhan outbreak, from which stories emerged of apartment buildings being sealed up, doors welded shut, barricades erected on the streets and sophisticated surveillance systems being deployed to monitor the movement of people (Wu, 2020). However, even in supposedly free societies like the UK and Australia, strict restrictions were imposed throughout much of 2020 and 2021 in the name of public health. It seems that:

> There is no return to normal, the new 'normal' will have to be constructed on the ruins of our old lives, or we will find ourselves in a new barbarism whose signs are already clearly discernible. It will not be enough to treat the epidemic as an unfortunate accident, to get rid of its consequences and return to the smooth functioning of the old way of doing things, with perhaps some adjustments to our healthcare arrangements. We will have to raise the key question: What is wrong with our system that we were caught unprepared by the catastrophe despite scientists warning us about it for years?
>
> *(Žižek, 2020, pp. 3–4)*

Early in the course of the pandemic, UN Secretary-General António Guterres warned that the COVID-19 pandemic would not simply be a public health crisis, but also an economic crisis and social crisis, claiming that the pandemic was 'a human crisis that is fast becoming a human rights crisis' (Guterres, 2020, np). While the focus of his arguments was on equitable access to quality healthcare, especially for people in areas of significant disadvantage, he warned that 'against the background of rising ethno-nationalism, populism, authoritarianism and a pushback against human rights in some countries, the crisis can provide a pretext to adopt repressive measures for purposes unrelated to the pandemic' (Guterres, 2020, np). The fault lines of precarity, poverty and unequal access to healthcare and education pre-existed the pandemic, although these have been widened and the effects have been disproportionately felt by marginalised and disadvantaged communities (Carr, 2020).

There has been a rapid increase in state and corporate surveillance, alongside the curtailing of civil liberties and restrictions on freedom of movement and association, which will be difficult to roll back once the public health argument of such control measures are no longer required. The use of more invasive policing and profiling of marginalised groups, as well as the increased uptake of surveillance technologies (e.g., iPhone scanning messages, thermal imaging, facial recognition software, number plate recognition and movement tracking) will take considerable public effort to be wound back. At the time of writing, roughly half of Australian citizens are under 'stay at home' orders, restricting freedom of movement and association. There are massive restrictions on international entry to Australia, with approximately 30,000 Australians stranded overseas and unable to return home for the past 18 months. In addition, the police and even army personnel have been used to enforce strict lockdown rules, disproportionately within communities with high levels of poverty, social disadvantage and speakers of languages other than English. The corrosive effects on social cohesion are apparent, with even progressive voices loudly declaring on social media to 'lock them down!' However, the restrictions are neither uniform nor equally enforced, which simply reinforces the growing divide between those that have and can, with those who have not and cannot.

Foucault's (2003) conception of biopolitics as the state's sovereignty over populations is useful to consider how governments have responded to the pandemic, in particular the policy choices over human bodies, where they can travel or be located (i.e., lockdowns and quarantines), who gets medical care (i.e., the rich and those in countries such as Australia with effective social healthcare), access to vaccines (i.e., not sub-Saharan African countries) and so on. The public debate around the approach to the pandemic has effectively been a struggle between those who seek government intervention through harsh biopolitical restrictions, including lockdowns, border closures, quarantine and so on, and those who pursue a more libertarian 'let it rip' strategy of non-intervention by the state. These discourses are often termed as 'living with the virus', although for many people, especially those who occupy precarious positions within society, the reality has been 'dying with the virus'. Of course, the binary argument that we must either choose life or the economy has been false the entire time (Lévy, 2020).

The pandemic has spurred on a global restructuring of capital, which is increasingly funnelling wealth to the few—especially the elite club of billionaires and eccentric entrepreneurs like Elon Musk and Jeff Bezos—while the many suffer increasing economic and health burdens of a system stacked against them. The pandemic 'is likely to heighten the concentration of capital worldwide and worsen social inequality. Enabled by digital applications, the ruling groups—unless they are pushed to change course by mass pressure from below—will turn to ratcheting up the global police state to contain the coming social upheavals' (Robinson, 2020, np). It seems that this ratcheting up of policing can be observed in the increased use of surveillance technologies and the use of police and military to ensure compliance with public health orders. As one example of many, a 'hard' border has been put in place between the Australian states of Queensland—where I live and work, and which is currently relatively free of COVID-19—and New South Wales, which is in the middle of a widespread outbreak and rapidly increasing cases, hospitalisations and deaths more than 18 months into the pandemic. The response of the Queensland government has been to restrict border movement even further, denying entry on compassionate grounds and even bringing in the military to help patrol the border crossings. If someone had told me a couple of years ago that I would be living in a state that placed police and military personnel on its border to ensure that no one crossed over, I would probably have laughed in disbelief that the liberal–democratic society in which I lived would rapidly move to a quasi-police state. Yet, here we are.

One favourite saying of politicians these past endless months has been to claim that 'we are all in the same boat', which was quickly modified by activists to 'we are all in the same storm, but we are not in the same boat'. The pandemic has exacerbated issues of social cohesion and laid bare the enormous disparity between the wealthy and poor, even in relatively rich Western countries like Australia, the US and UK. Žižek (2020) argued that 'a common sooth now in circulation is that, since we are all now in this crisis together, we should forget about politics and just work in unison to save ourselves. This notion is false: true politics are needed now—decisions about solidarity are eminently political' (p. 94). However, there have been few moments at which something approaching true politics has emerged during the pandemic. As Lipscy (2020) argued, it is likely that COVID-19 was labelled as a global health crisis due to the 'high concentration of early casualties in Western states, reflecting implicit judgements about the relative importance of states and populations in the international system' (p. E114).

El-Erian (2021) warned that the unequal global rollout of vaccines has weakened trust in the international system, which must be taken seriously by Western democratic powers like the US and UK because, 'with no other multilateral system to replace the current one, the only alternative is a scenario of global fragmentation and rising economic, social and political tensions' (np). Further, Lipscy (2020) explained:

> COVID has highlighted and exacerbated long-simmering income and racial disparities. The crisis provides an opportunity for governments to experiment with radical policy shifts, such as a universal basic income or a Green New Deal. It may also turn the global tide against populism and soft-authoritarianism, as leaders like Donald Trump and Jair Bolsonaro demonstrate the pitfalls of ignoring scientific expertise in favor of nativism and tabloid conspiracy theories. However, the pandemic also provides a pretext to justify unprecedented intrusions into the daily lives of citizens, which can strengthen the hand of autocrats and further erode democratic institutions.
>
> *(p. E120)*

The threshold at which we find ourselves during the COVID-19 pandemic is critical for how the remaining decades of the twenty-first century might play out. There is potential for the continued erosion of democratic principles and institutions as high-tech surveillance becomes ubiquitous and governments continue to impose restrictions on civil liberties such as freedom of movement and association, all in the name of protecting the population against themselves. For example, the emergent introduction of vaccine passports in many places around the world will likely have unintended consequences for privacy, freedom and participation within society. Conversely, it is possible that more radical democratic forms may emerge from the crisis, and that a reclaiming of the public good, whether that is public health or public education, will take a prime position in policymaking, alongside meaningful climate change action and the addressing of social and economic inequalities.

Lévy (2020) argued that we should avoid making claims that the pandemic is a learning experience or an opportunity to become better, given that the virus holds no particular views on the well-being of humanity, and despite the hyperventilating claims of some evangelical preachers, the virus is not some divine punishment in judgement of our sins. Similarly, Žižek (2020) argued that 'we should resist the temptation to treat the ongoing epidemic as something that has a deeper meaning: the cruel but just punishment of humanity for the ruthless exploitation of other forms of life on earth' (p. 14). However, perhaps one useful observation we can make is that 'we never spend enough, anywhere, for research teams or hospitals' (Lévy, 2020, p. 35).

The COVID-19 pandemic has demonstrably been a 'great unequaliser' globally, which has 'compounded disparities in income, wealth and opportunity. It has laid bare for all to see not only the vast numbers of people in the world who are economically and socially vulnerable, but also the depth and degree of their fragility' (Schwab & Malleret, 2020, p. 59). The pandemic has highlighted the inexcusable inequality between those that have and those that do not, exposing the weaknesses along classed, gendered, raced and state-based lines. Those who were classified as *essential workers* during lockdowns—unable to work from home and required to face the daily threat of infection, sickness and death—strongly overlaid those who work in precarious, low-paid jobs such as retail, transportation, health and social services. They were the nurses, aged care and disability carers, factory workers, warehouse staff and delivery drivers. Underpaid, overworked and placed in positions of extreme risk, it became apparent that those whom society most relies upon to function are those who are least regarded or rewarded economically, socially and politically.

Much remains to be understood about the pandemic, although the scholarly community is rapidly doing its work. A simple Google Scholar search for publications during 2020 and 2021 with the search 'covid OR pandemic OR COVID-19 OR coronavirus' returned over 425,000 results. A standard Google search for the same terms over the same time returned over 2.6 billion results. Evidently, there is much interest in writing and thinking about the pandemic, although it is likely that much of the information generated in response is questionable at best, through to deliberate misinformation and lies generated to sow fear and distrust.

Truth and Trust in the Age of Trump

> The ongoing spread of the coronavirus epidemic has also triggered a vast epidemic of ideological viruses which were lying dormant in our societies: fake news, paranoiac conspiracy theories, explosions of racism. The well-grounded medical need for quarantines found an echo in the ideological pressure to establish clear borders and to quarantine enemies who pose a threat to our identity.
>
> *(Žižek, 2020, p. 39)*

Postmodernism has long been criticised by some as heralding the death of truth, with its positioning of subjectivity at the heart of human knowledge and experience, alongside its critique of language as always being partial and malleable. So, it was unsurprising that when the Oxford Dictionary named 'post-truth' as its word of the year in 2016, many scholars and commentators claimed that it was proof that postmodernism had finally conquered scientific rationality and reason, overriding some objective truth with preference for alternative facts that were more closely aligned with personal ideologies (McIntyre, 2018). However, such critiques have been misguided in their assumption that there's a coherent epistemological theory driving the emergence and uptake of post-truth discourses. On the contrary, the emergence of a post-truth politics has been a long time coming, and is driven by a complex array of factors, not the least of which is growing mistrust in democracy and democratic institutions.

Bauman (2017) cautioned that without trust, the bonds of human commitment to each other fall apart, replaced by fear and loathing, which becomes 'self-reproducing, self-corroborating and self-magnifying' (p. 92). In its place, 'trust is replaced by universal suspicion. All bonds are assumed to be untrustworthy, unreliable, trap-and-ambush-like—until proven otherwise; but in the absence of trust the very idea of a "proof", let alone a clinching and final proof, is anything but clear and convincing' (Bauman, 2017, p. 92). This is not an outcome of postmodern and poststructural theories, but rather the culmination of a long-running series of erosions of a commitment to the notion of the public, by corporations and governments of all persuasions across much of the liberal–democratic world.

The erosion of trust and stoking of hate and fear is a deliberate strategy of authoritarian and populist demagogues, alongside the mythologising of an imaginary 'pure citizenry' to pursue agendas of exclusion and oppression. Verma and Apple (2021) argued that the use of mistrust, fear and hate in political rhetoric enables them to gain traction as acceptable responses, and that in liberal–democratic nations, when political 'leaders are elected that employ hate and racist nativism as a cornerstone of their agenda, complicated and dangerous articulations of hate are normalized in everyday common sense' (p. 7). Such normalisation and making common of fear and hate are amplified and exacerbated by social media, such as the rise of hate groups and hate speech on Facebook (Vaidhyanathan, 2018).

Further, despite the promise that the growth of electronic communications and instant digital connection might 'create an informed public more capable of self-government than ever before in history, fake news, hate speech, and "alternative facts" have seriously degraded the civic discourse' (Gardels & Berggruen, 2019, pp. 2–3). The powerful influence of misinformation and fear amplified via social media platforms has created massive disruption to the flow of information and the production of 'truth' and 'knowledge'. Vaidhyanathan (2018) claimed that the ubiquity of Facebook as a social media platform has caused more division and harm than social good, in which 'the idealistic vision of people sharing more information with ever more people has not improved nations or global culture, enhanced mutual understanding, or strengthened democratic movements' (p. 4). Vaidhyanathan (2018) argued:

> The autocrat, the de-territorialized terrorist organization, the insurgent group, the prankster, and the internet troll share a relationship to the truth: they see it as beside the point. If they can get the rest of us scrambling to find our balance, they have achieved their goals. Those who oppose or dismiss democracy and the deliberation and debate that make democracy possible do not care whether claims are true or false, or even how widely they are accepted as true. What matters is that a loud voice disrupts the flow of discourse, and that all further argument will be centered on the truth of the claim itself rather than on a substantive engagement with facts. Power is all that matters when trust and truth crumble.
>
> (p. 13)

Lee (2015) argued that each political ideology—such as liberal–democratic capitalism, socialism, fascism or other forms of authoritarianism—takes up particular claims about what is 'true' and positions them according to a coherent logic that is specific to that ideology. What may appear to be incoherent to an outsider, does in fact adhere to a fairly rigorous internal rationality to the insider. This is why those who adhere to certain conspiracy theories and extremist ideologies are so difficult to persuade to think otherwise. Likewise, governments, corporations and other powerful institutions 'operate within their own reality, motivated by a combination of self-interest, national interest (sometimes), ideology, and a desire to maintain the power and positions they hold' (Lee, 2015, p. 2). These regimes of truth (Foucault, 2003) work to ensure that the powerful, particularly the corporate oligarchy supported by the political class, are able to avoid scrutiny and opposition, by ensuring that the democratic impulse is redirected and the populace is distracted. Giroux (2009) argued that there is a deliberate devaluing of the role of citizens, civic values and democratic power, so that communal responsibility gives way to distrust, fear and loathing.

Speaking with Jeffrey Goldberg, editor of *The Atlantic*, former US president Barack Obama opined that 'if we do not have the capacity to distinguish what's true from what's false, then by definition the marketplace of ideas doesn't work. And by definition our democracy doesn't work. We are entering into an epistemological crisis' (Obama, as cited in Goldberg, 2020). There is little doubt that we face a significant epistemic crisis, in which truth and knowledge are weaponised and turned upon the polity, whether through overt acts such as Trump's attempted coup in early 2021, which was framed as a patriotic duty to 'stop the steal', or via the slower but potentially more insidious rhetoric and discursive strategies deployed in conspiracy theory social media groups. Further, Vaidhyanathan (2018) argued that:

> Those who study or follow the rise of authoritarianism and the alarming erosion of democracy around the world would by 2017 list India, Indonesia, Kenya, Poland, Hungary, and the United States as sites of Facebook's direct contribution to violent ethnic and religious nationalism, the rise of authoritarian leaders, and a sort of mediated cacophony that would hinder public deliberation about important issues, thus undermining trust in institutions and experts.
>
> *(p. 2)*

Mistrust in experts and expertise can be observed in the rise of the anti-vaccination movement around the globe—which is having a dangerously chilling effect on vaccination rates and thus, perpetuating the misery and suffering caused by the pandemic—alongside rapid growth in conspiracy theories from the mundane to the ridiculous, yet dangerous cult of QAnon. And these conspiracies and mistrust in expertise are encouraged and amplified by those in political positions of power who should, and generally do, know better. For example, in the lead-up to the Brexit referendum, conservative British politician Michael Gove claimed that 'I think the people of this country have had enough of experts with organisations with acronyms saying that they know what is best' (Gove, as cited in

Mance, 2016). Similarly, Trump made his disdain for experts abundantly clear on the 2016 presidential campaign trail, when he declared that 'the experts are terrible. Look at the mess we're in with all these experts that we have. Look at the mess' (Trump, as cited in Gass, 2016).

In addition, Zakaria (2020) argued that the rapid growth of anti-elitism and distrust in experts and institutions is a reflection of the sense of powerlessness and alienation experienced by many people as a result of the material and social effects of poverty, employment precarity and social division. When hurting, people seek for someone to blame, and intellectuals and experts have always been a target of choice. After all, their job is to make things better, so why then do things keep getting worse? The feelings of alienation often have limited avenues for expression beyond a general affective atmosphere of distrust and simmering resentment on social media. Although, when they spill over into the world-at-large, the effects can be calamitous. Gerrard (2021) argued that the contemporary debates regarding the global rise of far-right extremism and populism clearly demonstrate that there is an urgent need to 'consider the ways in which knowledge and the claim to authority and expertise are invariably wrapped within collective politics, capitalist inequality, and alienation from "traditional" expertise' (p. 165).

One example of the spill over of resentment and alienation can be observed in the toxic discourse in the lead-up to the UK's 'Brexit' referendum in June 2016, as well as the political rhetoric and public debate following the referendum to the eventual withdrawal from the EU on 31 January 2020. Euroscepticism had long been a feature of UK political discourse, which combined with growing anti-immigration sentiment following the increase in asylum seeker movement across the Mediterranean over the past two decades, stoked by right-wing commentators and political actors who based their rhetoric on racist and xenophobic tropes (Evans & Mellon, 2019; Vasilopoulou, 2016). A complex set of factors were responsible for the Brexit outcome, although much can be levelled at the crushing effects of economic and social inequalities and the fermenting of post-truth discourses (Dorling, 2019).

In the US, the era of Trump as president may have come to its ignominious conclusion in the failed coup of February 2021, but Trumpism as a political and social force is far from over. It is important to understand the conditions under which a predatory property developer and self-aggrandising opportunist like Trump was able to dominate the political stage in the lead-up to the 2016 presidential election, first taking the Republican nomination, then eventually winning the presidency by virtue of an electoral system that provides unequal distribution of voting power, and then running his administration via incoherent ranting on his personal Twitter account for the following four years.

Clearly, Trump was not the source of the issues facing the US polity, but rather was symptomatic of long-running tensions and resentments that drew on historical currents of racism, exclusion and poverty, woven with class and race politics, and fuelled by growing extremism and polarisation. In particular,

Trump was fond of courting White supremacists and neofascist groups, drawing them together with the MAGA crowd, who sought an outlet for their disaffection and disenfranchisement (De Genova, 2020). However, Trump has entrenched an anti-democratic culture that will have long-lasting effects, through 'his court appointments, in his creation of a solid minority of at least 45 percent animated by resentment and revenge, but above all in his unabashed demonstration of the relatively unbounded possibilities of an American autocracy' (O'Toole, 2020, np). Trump could be described as a pluto-populist who wished to instil himself as a capitalist authoritarian demagogue in the vein of Russia's Putin, Turkey's Erdoğan or Brazil's Bolsonaro (Wolf, 2020), although thankfully the democratic and liberal institutions of the US managed to prevent him from staging a successful coup in January 2021. However, what comes next for Trumpism after Trump could be much more dire for the US and the world.

Further, Hopkin and Blyth (2020) claimed that Trumpism can be understood as a global phenomenon, in which there has been widespread backlash against the neoliberal business-as-usual of Western liberal capitalist democracies, particularly against the widening of social and economic inequalities that is a persistent feature of such systems. The effects of a politics of resentment observed in the UK's Brexit and Trump's US can be traced back to the neoliberal economic and social policies of the past several decades, with its roots in the powerful influence of Hayek, Thatcher and Reagan on economic policymaking. The end result is a population that has separated from a sense of civic responsibility and duty to care for each other, leaving an atomised and highly untrusting set of social groups, who struggle to find common cause in a time of precarity, pandemic and rising authoritarian populism.

At the heart of the current crisis of truth and trust is the powerful effects of language being manipulated and corrupted through the rise of alternative facts and post-truth epistemologies. In his essay, *Politics and the English Language*, Orwell (1946) argued that political language 'is designed to make lies sound truthful and murder respectable, and to give an appearance of solidity to pure wind' (p. 265). While political actors have long used the language of persuasion to further their agendas, the hyper-activation of conspiracies, wildly inaccurate claims and fake news have proliferated to levels previously unthinkable on platforms such as Facebook and Twitter, to the point where fake news and alternative facts have become direct threats to democratic values and intellectual culture (Vaidhyanathan, 2018).

Truth and democracy cannot be separated from each other because the polity must be able to trust its political institutions and leaders. However, when political deceit becomes commonplace and trust is eroded, there is irreparable harm done to the bonds of loyalty to the state, which Osborne (2021) argued can open the way to anarchy and political dispossession. It is important that there is trust for democracy to work because trust 'represents an expansion of legitimacy, in that it adds to a mere procedural attribute both a moral dimension (integrity in the broadest sense) and a substantive dimension (concern for the common good).

Trust also plays a temporal role: it implies that the expansion of legitimacy continues into the future' (Rosenvallon, 2017, p. 3). When trust gives way to distrust in political institutions and social norms, legitimacy suffers and we enter into what Rosenvallon (2017) called the *society of distrust*, which has significant implications for social cohesion, political engagement and commitment to the collective good. As Tukekci (2020) argued, democratic 'institutions rely on people collectively agreeing to act in a certain way. Human laws do not simply exert their power like the inexorable pull of gravity. Once people decide that the rules are different, the rules are different. The rules for electoral legitimacy have been under sustained assault, and they're changing right before our eyes' (Tukekci, 2020).

One clear example of the dangerous effects of the *society of distrust* can be observed in the Trump presidency from 2017 to the beginning of 2021, in which a key theme was social division and stoking racial and class-based prejudices, the flagrant disdain for democratic norms and ideals, alongside the wholesale reshaping of truth to suit the political desires of Trump, his immediate supporters within his administration and the Republican party, as well as the broader base who voted him into power and enthusiastically cheered on each brazen act. O'Toole (2020) provided the following salient insights:

> The Trump presidency has been no nightmare. It has been daylight delinquency, its transgressions of democratic values on lurid display in all their corruption and cruelty and deadly incompetence. There may be much we do not yet know, but what is known (and in most cases openly flaunted) is more than enough: the Mueller report, the Ukraine scandal, the flagrant self-dealing, the tax evasion, the children stolen from their parents, the encouragement of neo-Nazis, Trump's admission that he deliberately played down the seriousness of the coronavirus. There can be no awakening because the Republicans did not sleep through all of this. They saw it all and let it happen. In electoral terms, moreover, it turns out that they were broadly right. There was no revulsion among the party base. The faithful not only witnessed his behavior, they heard Trump say, repeatedly, that he would not accept the result of the vote. They embraced that authoritarianism with renewed enthusiasm. The assault on democracy now has a genuine, highly engaged, democratic movement behind it.
>
> *(np)*

Tukekci (2020) warned that the stage has been set for a smarter, more coherent and organised autocrat to sweep into power in the future, aided and abetted by the minoritarian rule and tacit approval of a captive Republican party, supported by the angry throated rage of a dispossessed and disposed class of White supremacist voters who have no other form to express their dismay at the loss of material and social wealth in a system that has sought to marginalise and then exploit their position. Arendt (1969) argued that when thoughts and reality part company, there is opportunity for explosive 'outbursts of passionate exasperation with reason, thought, and rational discourse' (p. 6). This is how a reality TV sleazebag like Trump was able to manipulate the political atmosphere of resentment and turn the society of distrust in the US against itself and towards his own personal empowerment and to fill his bank account, those of his closest allies and his companies. Trump may now be out of the White House, but Trumpism has a long way yet to play out its narrative.

A further example of the erosion of truth and trust can be observed in the rapid explosion of conspiracy theories, from anti-vaccination social media groups, 'Sovereign Citizen' protests against COVID-19 restrictions, through to the more dangerous behaviours displayed by some QAnon adherents, religious fundamentalists, White supremacists and radicalised militia members. For example, a recent survey found that 39 per cent of Australians believed that the COVID-19 pandemic was deliberately engineered and released by the Chinese government in a Wuhan laboratory, while 19 per cent believed that Bill Gates had played a role in the creation and spread of the pandemic, and 12 per cent believed that 5G was used to spread the virus (McGowan, 2021). Perhaps one could laugh these off as the 'gullible rump' of society, yet there is an insistence and persistence of such views, which quickly leak into mainstream discourses. For example, there are members of parliament in the current federal government who actively spruik anti-vaccination rhetoric and promote the use of dangerous alternative treatments for COVID-19 on social media.

The basic premise of the QAnon conspiracy, which has gained an enormous worldwide following, is that there is a secret cabal of Satan-worshipping Democrats, celebrities and billionaires who are really running the world (Wong, 2020). Further, QAnon adherents believe in the 'deep state' as a secret form of super-government, which seeks to control the world. They considered Trump to be a hero in the narrative, as someone who waging war against the deep state in his promise to 'drain the swamp'. The emergence and proliferation of QAnon has fuelled 'the growth of a lurid meta-conspiracy connecting a range of harmful narratives. The QAnon theory now connects antivaccine, anti-5G conspiracies, antisemitic and antimigrant tropes, and several bizarre theories that the world is in the thrall of a group of paedophile elites set on global domination in part aided by ritualistic child sacrifice' (Gallagher et al., 2020, p. 3). The rise of such conspiracies points to the continuing erosion of truth and trust, which has serious implications for the future of democracy. There are also implications for the rise of populism and anti-democratic sentiment, in which the people are poisoned by post-truth politics and brought to support demagogues and authoritarian leaders under a series of false promises.

Populism and a Poisoned People

Something is happening. 'Anti-establishment', 'anti-system', 'anti-elite', 'populist' sentiments are exploding in many mature democracies. After almost a century during which the same parties dominated democratic politics, new parties are springing up like mushrooms while the support for traditional ones is dwindling. Electoral participation is declining in many countries to historically unprecedented levels. Confidence in politicians, parties, parliaments, and governments is falling. Even the support for democracy as a system of government has weakened. Popular preferences about policies diverge sharply. Moreover, the symptoms are not just political. Loss of confidence in institutions extends to the media, banks, private corporations, even churches. People with different political views, values, and cultures increasingly view each other as enemies. They are willing to do nasty things to each other.

(Przeworski, 2019, p. 1)

In Chapter 2, some of the contemporary challenges facing liberal democracy were outlined, with an emphasis on the effects of how neoliberalism and capitalism have eroded the notion of the public good, replacing it with private pursuits and an atomised populace. We sit at a threshold, which will determine how the coming decades play out. The intersections of neoliberalism, an eroded public sphere, a global pandemic and the rise of anti-democratic and populist sentiments are yet to be fully realised, but the challenge is manifest. Moffitt and Tormey (2014) claimed that the contemporary political landscape has progressively become more performative and stylised, which has provided fertile ground for the growth of populist modes of political discourse. Further, Moffitt (2016) argued that the global rise of populism is intertwined with the intense mediatisation of communication technologies such as 24-hour news cycle and social media, and that populism is a performative political style, in which the aesthetic and relational elements combine with rhetorical and discursive strategies. The ubiquitous reach of social media, especially the Facebook and Twitter platforms, has served to amplify and extend the messaging of populist actors. Vaidhyanathan (2018) suggested that 'if you wanted to design a media system to support authoritarian leaders and anti-democratic movements, you could not do much better than Facebook' (p. 186), which has been at the centre of a worldwide digital assault on democracy.

Within a context of increasing pessimism and widening inequality, it is not surprising that people would seek an outlet for their frustrations. However, the hegemonic systems of representative democracy that seek to serve the interests of the corporate oligarchs and political class have consistently offered no real solutions for people struggling to survive, let alone thrive, in contemporary capitalist societies. Indeed, Srnicek and Williams (2016) argued that capitalism necessarily produces 'surplus' populations (e.g., those who are unemployed or underemployed, women, children and minorities) and that the process is being accelerated by automation and globalisation. Consumerist culture is a poor replacement for meaningful engagement in public life, and the gnawing discontent can be observed in the growing levels of distrust and fear that puncture our social and political discourses. Technological disruption continues apace, further disenfranchising those who are already on the margins, creating additional 'surplus' populations. It has become clear that 'the very social basis of capitalism as an economic system—the relationship between the proletariat and employers, with waged work mediating between them—is crumbling' (Srnicek & Williams, 2016, p. 92). Yet, there is nothing in place as a viable alternative to the destructive appetites of capitalism, prompting the warning:

> As the hegemonic order predicated upon decent and stable jobs breaks down, social control is likely to revert to increasingly coercive measures: harsher workfare, heightened antagonisms over immigration, stricter controls on the movement of peoples, and mass incarceration for those who resist being cast aside. This is the crisis of work facing neoliberalism and the surplus populations who make up most of the world's labour force.
> *(Srnicek & Williams, 2016, p. 104)*

The current context is ripe for the fermentation of anti-democratic sentiment and the rise of populist and authoritarian demagogues. Trump is one example of a populist demagogue leader who has effectively played a deceptive yet compelling political tune for 'the people', but there are many others, from Brazil's Jair Bolsonaro, India's Narendra Modi, Turkey's Recep Tayyip Erdoğan, Belarus' Alexander Lukashenko, Russia's Vladimir Putin, to The Philippines' Rodrigo Duterte. There are countless others, including folk like Pauline Hanson and her One Nation party in Australia, who seek to evoke populist modes of anger, resentment and fear. Despite having a wide variety of political beliefs and ends, each of these populist actors attempt to evoke 'the people', rely on a pessimistic narrative of external and internal threats (e.g., immigrants, homosexuals and Jewish people), the disregard of political and social norms, a neo-conservative view of the family and society as being under attack by progressive forces, the deployment of political incorrectness, shock and offence (Moffitt & Tormey, 2014, p. 389).

Moffitt (2016) claimed that populists have been successful in their strategy to set 'the people' against 'the elite' in the cause of a popular sovereignty and defence of democracy. Invariably, the argument is made that the experts are the enemy, and they have caused the economic, social and political dispossession and disenfranchisement of the people. It is devastatingly effective, given the groundwork has already been laid through the work of neoliberalism and capitalism on hollowing out the public, while leaving people in precarity and poverty, alongside the rise of mistrust in expertise, explosion of conspiracies and alternative facts and the pernicious effects of deliberate misinformation, propaganda and political spin. Writing some 45 years ago, Laclau (1977) claimed:

> The emergence of populism is historically linked to a crisis of the dominant ideological discourse which is in turn part of a more general social crisis. This crisis can either be the result of a fracture in the power bloc,

in which a class or class fraction needs, in order to assert its hegemony, to appeal to 'the people' against established ideology as a whole; or of a crisis in the ability of the system to neutralise the dominated sectors—that is to say, a crisis of transformism.

(Laclau, 1977, p. 175)

The increasing sway of populism in the context of collapsing ecological, economic, social and political systems in the first two decades of the twenty-first century can be understood as a fairly logical rejection of the hegemonic discourses of neoliberalism and capitalism. Laclau (2005) conceived of populism as being a political logic of extreme collective will, which becomes manifested through the emergence of a dangerous excess energy of the 'crowd'. This is what makes it so appealing to demagogues and authoritarians. By tapping into and harnessing the excess energy of the crowd, the populist leader is able to make sweeping changes in the name of a popular mandate. Of course, populism is not intrinsically good or bad, but has been 'described as both a democratic threat and a democratic corrective' (Sant, 2021, p. 57). Think of the polarisation of extreme right-wing discourses behind Donald Trump during the 2016 presidential primaries, against those of far left-wing discourses behind Bernie Sanders.

Moffitt (2016) argued that populism is no longer a fringe political phenomenon, but has become a 'mainstay of contemporary politics across the globe' (p. 2). At its core is a deep antipathy towards the establishment (Zakaria, 2020), which includes the political class, experts and those who are seen as possessing economic and cultural power. Populist actors seek to establish arbitrary binary relationships between 'us' (i.e., the people) and 'them' (i.e., anyone who falls outside of the parameters of membership of the people), radically simplifying issues to black-and-white terms with quick political fixes that appear to present them as strong and decisive leaders, often in contrast to their actions (Moffitt, 2015).

Importantly, Rosenvallon (2017) argued that 'populists have no interest in fighting on the usual political battlegrounds. Instead, they warn of decadence and pose as guardians of purity, saviors of the nation from political extremes, and prophets of an apocalypse from which they will emerge victorious' (p. 271). The power of populism is in its ability to mobilise the image of a homogenous and unified people, with the strident rejection of any who threaten the homogeneity. The popularity of populism lies in its rejection of technocrats, experts and institutions in the name of the people (Bloom & Sancino, 2019). The people who are most exploited by populists are those who have been impoverished by contemporary capitalism and neoliberal policies, left marginalised and disenfranchised by a system that does not benefit them (Schostak & Goodson, 2020). As such, resentment, anger and fear are the key drivers of populist movements, with significant consequences.

Populists manipulate a performance of perpetual crisis, in which they pit the people against those who have created the crisis, often using deception and propaganda to amplify and exaggerate their claims, before presenting overly simplified solutions that have the appearance of strong and decisive leadership, yet do not offer the people any real succour or increase in power and wealth (Moffitt, 2015). Populists deploy emotive and morally vilifying language, which is less about making sense on a rational, cognitive level, and more about connecting with people on the affective register. Populism 'knows how to stoke anger and stir protest in the streets and voting booths. Populism's rising power reflects the fact that negative sovereignty finds itself imprisoned in the immediate: it is a force radically bereft of ideas, incapable of active criticism, and reduced to the expression of resigned violence' (Rosenvallon, 2017, p. 271).

Rather than an anomaly arising from unforeseen circumstances, Temelkuran (2019) argued that populism is the 'mutant child of crippled representative democracy' (p. 23). The response of mainstream political discourse to reduce the problem of populism as being akin to dealing with a naughty toddler (e.g., Trump) and the confused, ignorant masses (e.g., people attending Trump's MAGA rallies) misunderstands the scale and severity of the problem and its threat to inclusive and caring forms of democracy (Temelkuran, 2019). Left unchecked, populism leads to authoritarianism modes of governance, with fascism and other totalitarian political forms enabled and strengthened as a result of the success of populism.

It seems that Arendt (1973, 1998), Laclau (1977, 2005) and Mouffe (1993, 2019) provide useful conceptual tools for understanding the ways in which populism, totalitarianism and fascism work to create perverse and corrupt forms of democracy. Argued in the name of the people, these forms rely upon a compliant public that is bound by mistrust and fear, in which truth can be bent to the will of the oligarchs or autocrats who seek to weaponise and deploy the power of the masses. Carefully crafted messaging and propaganda are essential tools for the populist and authoritarian, who ensures that they are always positioned as the strong leader, defending the people from the evils from within and without.

Interestingly, Arendt (1973) argued that 'the ideal subject of totalitarian rule is not the convinced Nazi or the convinced Communist, but people for whom the distinction between fact and fiction (i.e., the reality of experience) and the distinction between true and false (i.e., the standards of thought) no longer exist' (p. 474). The current post-truth moment is one in which the boundaries between fact and fiction, true and false have largely become meaningless, replaced instead by an emphasis on how something makes one feel. Within this context, propaganda is powerfully effective because the 'masses do not trust their eyes and ears but only their imaginations, which may be caught by anything that is at once universal and consistent in itself. What convinces masses are not facts, and not even invented facts, but only the consistency of the system of which they are presumably part' (Arendt, 1973, p. 351). Think of the MAGA crowd. No matter how offensive or absurd Trump was during his stint in the White House, they simply adored him even more.

Further, the emergence of 'totalitarian movements depended less on the structurelessness of a mass society than on the specific conditions of an atomized and individualized mass' (Arendt, 1973, p. 318). More than three decades of neoliberalisation and globalised capitalism have produced the massified individualism of contemporary democracy (Rancière, 2006), which is ripe for the proliferation of new forms of fascist and other totalitarian regimes. Laclau (1977) argued that the transition to fascism is precipitated by a political crisis that breaks representational ties between the people and the political class, alongside a 'crisis of dominant ideology which develops into a generalized ideological crisis' (p. 90). Fascism thus emerges as the hegemony of oligarchic capital, supported by the extreme cultural and social polarisation effected by the political class to ensure that the population is distracted.

One is reminded of the argument, presented nearly a century ago by Counts (1932), that the political 'choice is no longer between individualism and collectivism. It is rather between two forms of collectivism: the one essentially democratic, the other feudal in spirit; the one devoted to the interests of the people, the other to the interests of a privileged class' (p. 49). While contemporary forms of populism that have emerged in liberal capitalist democracies may not be fully fascistic, they have within them the capacity to become so. The key is to counter and resist the further atomisation and isolation of individuals, who are then susceptible to the appeal of populist and totalitarian movements (Arendt, 1973), through the realisation of more inclusive and collective forms of democratic participation.

In response to the tendency for atomisation and mass individualism to tend towards populism, Mouffe (1999) argued for more pluralist forms of democracy, which are agonistic in their nature, as a bulwark against the splintering and destabilising slide from populist politics into totalitarianism. Further, 'the novelty of democratic politics is not the overcoming of this us/them distinction—which is what a consensus without exclusion pretends to achieve—but the different way in which is established. What is at stake is how to establish the us/them discrimination in a way that is compatible with pluralist democracy' (Mouffe, 1999, p. 755). Mouffe's (2019) argument was that a productive agonistic and pluralist democracy was most likely to provide a sustainable and lasting democratic sentiment. Similarly, Rancière's (2010) argument was that dissensus, not consensus, would generate a more inclusive and productive democracy.

Further, Mouffe (1993) urged to abandon the illusion of consensus and unanimity because they fail to ensure a political frontier and are fatal to democracy. She argued that 'the absence of a political frontier, far from being a sign of political maturity, is the symptom of a void that can endanger democracy, because that void provides a terrain that can be occupied by the extreme right to articulate new anti-democratic political identities' (Mouffe, 1993, p. 5). Our current context is ripe for authoritarian and totalitarian forms of politics, given the atomisation of individuals and the erosion of the notion of public good and commitment to civic discourses through the hyper-competitive and individualised policies of neoliberalism and the caustic effects of globalised oligarchic capitalism. However, rather than reverting to some earlier form of democratic modes of governance, Mouffe (2019) instead suggested that a left populism could provide a more productive political frontier in response to the unfolding crises:

> In the next few years, I argue, the central axis of the political conflict will be between right-wing populism and left-wing populism. And as a result, it is through the construction of a 'people', a collective will that results from the mobilization of common affects in defence of equality and social justice, that it will be possible to combat the xenophobic policies promoted by right-wing populism.
>
> *(p. 6)*

For Mouffe (2019), a commitment to left populism recovers and deepens the 'ideals of equality and popular sovereignty that are constitutive of a democratic politics' (p. 9). Further, the notion of a left populism considers the collective will to reimagine the public in the interest of the commons, rather than the corporate oligarchs and political class. For Rancière (2010), this is achieved through the casting aside of current forms of neoliberal capitalist democracy that promote massified individualism and selfish consumerism, instead reimagining democracy as a mode of encounter between people who are equals within communities for a common purpose, rather than for generating inequality, exploitation and oppression.

Schooling as Inoculation Against Fear and Hate

We are living in a time when communal bonds are under strain or coming apart, when social media exacerbates the growing resentment, mistrust, fear and hate, and when particular forms of right-wing, xenophobic and neofascistic populism are on the rise in many liberal democracies. Global capitalism and the attendant neoliberal policies of the past decades have widened social and economic inequalities to unsustainable levels, with people facing an uncertain and precarious future. Amid all of this, we are living through a global pandemic that has wrought devastation and suffering, although this has been unequally experienced, disproportionately affecting those who are marginalised and disenfranchised by our political, economic and social systems.

This brings us to the question that this book takes as its central focus: In a time of multiple intersecting global crises, what could be the response of schooling to help generate more inclusive and caring forms of democratic participation and commitment to the public good? How can schooling be *for* democracy in ways that support and nurture young people to be informed, capable, critical and creative citizens that work collaboratively on the big problems of this century? There is no easy, straightforward answer, but perhaps one response is to consider the various issues of post-truth, alternative facts, hate speech, White supremacy, racism, misogyny, violence, mistrust, fear and loathing as being of a viral nature, not dissimilar to a coronavirus. One of our most powerful tools to counter the harm caused by a viral epidemic is to undertake widespread inoculation programs, using purpose-designed vaccines to protect people against infection, disease and death. Similarly, I suggest that schooling and other sites of education could provide social inoculation against the viruses of fear and misinformation.

Schwab and Malleret (2020) argued that social unrest will be one of the most profound dangers during the post-pandemic era, which could potentially lead to the disintegration of the bonds that hold societies together, alongside the collapse of political and economic institutions and structures. Their warning must be heeded, given that we are watching the slow unravelling of liberal democracy across the globe in real time. To hope that things will return to some new kind of normal once the immediacy of the horror of COVID-19 has receded is wishful thinking. Deliberate, active intervention is required, and teachers, schools and young people must be placed at the centre of the possibilities for reimagining education for democracy (Riddle & Apple, 2019). In the current neoliberal imaginary, young people are viewed as a problem, either cast as consumers and a workforce-in-waiting or as dangerous and reckless, requiring correction and compliance within the norms of globalised capitalism and the façade of democratic participation (Giroux, 2009). Young people are dangerous, and so they should be. After all, they contain within them the potential of a radically different society.

However, it is important to note that Gerrard (2021) observed that progressive education has assumed a false promise of education as being a site for improving social mobility, although the structural parameters of global and neoliberal capitalism continue to ensure that there are some who have access and opportunity, while others do not. There is a tension in the idea that 'more' education or 'better' education can act as a bulwark against the threats of populism, alternative facts, conspiracy theories and so on. As Gerrard (2021) explained, the conjuring of the educated (i.e., progressive, science-valuing and informed citizen) against the spectre of the abject uneducated, or in Hillary Clinton's words, 'the deplorables', raises 'significant questions surrounding what it is to know, who is understood as knowing, and the role of knowledge in contemporary capitalism' (p. 155).

The epistemic crisis that has arisen through the widespread proliferation of post-truth discourses, alternative facts, conspiracy theories and deliberate disinformation and misinformation should not be underestimated. Populist demagogues like Trump and Bolsanaro, along with the backlash politics of Brexit and growing right-wing and White supremacy movements, are all fuelled by the context of mistrust and fear. It would be trite to claim that ensuring everyone is educated would make the difference because that would fall into the trap of assuming that the issue is one of ignorance or lack of education, which is not the case. Instead, we need to consider which factors bring these anti-democratic and dangerous articulations of massified resentment and fear into a coalescent populism, and then configure how schooling and education could provide young people with evidence-based knowledge, scientific and sociological reasoning, and a critical thinking apparatus that works against the unknowing, uncaring effects of populist discourses (Sant & Brown, 2020).

However, our present schooling systems leave much to be desired. The concept of free, secular and universal public education has been at work for well over a century in liberal democracies, yet they remain far from equal in the access and opportunities provided to young people to engage in education. For example, Gardels and Berggruen (2019) described how the very concept of universal public education has become a classed and raced experience, while the children of the rich and powerful spend their days in elite private schools, which reinforces social and economic inequalities, segregating young people into groups that perpetuate the ongoing social division. The promise of education as a great equaliser has not been realised, but that does not mean that it should be abandoned. Instead, educators, parents, students and school leaders should seek ways to engage in more democratic and inclusive practices within schools, which support and extend the democratic project more broadly.

Curriculum should be explicitly anti-racist, anti-classist, anti-totalitarian and anti-populist. However, there is also a danger in the liberal and capitalist conception of education as a process of emancipation, in which the end goal is to be a productive member of the global workforce and a dutiful consumer citizen, who votes each election for this or that candidate, without addressing any of the underlying and systemic inequalities that permeate education. Sant and Brown (2020) cautioned against the universalising principles of liberal capitalist education that purports to be anti-populist, in which it gets trapped within a 'narrow understanding of these principles, specifically, a modernist form of education that does not allow other forms of thinking, experiencing or conceptualising' (p. 13).

A curriculum that takes anti-democratic sentiments head on must understand and bear witness to how the proliferation of hate and fear has enabled the spread of populist and authoritarian forms of political discourse, divided people from each other and supported the continued theft of wealth and power by the few. Verma and Apple (2021) argued that an honest appraisal of the dangerous articulations of social and cultural truths, expressed through fear and hate, provides 'a foundation for the next step, for engaging with the multiple ways in which disruption can take place in classrooms, communities, and nation-states. Combining the dual commitment to understanding and interruption is crucial, especially in schools and other pedagogic sites' (p. 10). Zembylas (2020) argued that an important part of the commitment of democratic education to tackle large social problems is to understand the affective dimensions of political and social thought, particularly the pedagogical implications arising from the discourses of fear and hate that permeate right-wing politics. Further, schooling that seeks to inoculate young people against the viruses of fear and hate must rest on the principle of radical equality, in which the democratic encounter can be realised between people who are equal and able to act collectively and collaboratively, within and without the classroom. Arendt (1973) reminded us that engagement in democratic political life requires the assumption of equality, although 'we are not born equal; we become equal as members of a group on the strength of our decision to guarantee ourselves mutually equal rights' (p. 301). Similarly, Rancière (2006) understood that democracy can only be realised in the encounter of equals, rather than something that becomes imposed upon a populace by governments, or when teachers exhort students to work together on problem-solving activities.

Carr (2020) argued that a functioning democracy is 'dependent on media/political literacy, critical engagement/participation, and the capacity to communicate, analyze, and disseminate nuanced perspectives, ideas, and information' (p. 4). This is where schools can play a vital role in providing young people with the skills and knowledge to be critical and creative participants in democratic life. However, as Carr (2020) warned, 'the quest to re-imagine a more meaningful, critically engaged democracy, especially during a context that is imbued with a political, economic, and public health crisis, cannot be delayed much longer' (p. 4).

Chapter 5 presents a more detailed series of propositions for schooling that extends and enables democracy, given the complex challenges facing young people. This chapter has outlined some of the contours of the COVID-19 pandemic alongside the virulent spread of mistrust, fear and hate through populist and authoritarian corruptions of the democratic impulse. Schooling cannot provide a panacea to these ills, but can offer an important and productive contribution to reshaping the social discourses, institutions and practices so that they are more inclusive, caring and sustainable than the current formations provided by global capitalism and neoliberal versions of liberal democracy. The path we are on is untenable, and the fraying is evident to those who care to look. We cannot afford to delay the reimagining of education and democracy because it is imperative that young people be supported as best as possible to tackle the great problems of the coming years and decades.

References

Albeck-Ripka, L., Tarabay, J., & Kwai, I. (2020, 4 January). As fires rage, Australia sees its leader as missing in action. *The New York Times*. https://www.nytimes.com/2020/01/04/world/australia/fires-scott-morrison.html

Arendt, H. (1969). *Between past and future: Eight exercises in political thought*. The Viking Press.

Arendt, H. (1973). *The origins of totalitarianism* (2nd ed.). Harcourt Brace & Company.

Arendt, H. (1998). *The human condition* (2nd ed.). University of Chicago Press.

Bauman, Z. (2017). *Wasted lives: Modernity and its outcasts*. Polity Press.

BBC. (2014). Are pandemics inevitable? *The Inquiry*. https://www.bbc.co.uk/sounds/play/p029kj9d

Bloom, P., & Sancino, A. (2019). *Disruptive democracy: The clash between techno-populism and techno-democracy*. Sage.

Carr, P. R. (2020). Shooting yourself first in the foot, then in the head: Normative democracy is suffocating, and then the coronavirus came to light. *Postdigital Science and Education*. https://doi.org/10.1007/s42438-020-00142-3

Connell, R. W. (2020). COVID-19/Sociology. *Journal of Sociology, 56*(4), 745–751. https://doi.org/10.1177/1440783320943262

Counts, G. S. (1932). *Dare the school build a new social order?* The John Day Company.
Cullen, W., Gulati, G., & Kelly, B. D. (2020). Mental health in the COVID-19 pandemic. *QJM: An International Journal of Medicine, 113*(5), 311–312. https://doi.org/10.1093/qjmed/hcaa110
Davis, H. E., Assaf, G. S., McCorkell, L., Wei, H., Low, R. J., Re'em, Y., Redfield, S., Austin, J. P., & Akrami, A. (2021). Characterizing long COVID in an international cohort: 7 months of symptoms and their impact. *EClinicalMedicine*. https://doi.org/10.1016/j.eclinm.2021.101019
De Genova, N. (2020). 'Everything is permitted': Trump, White supremacy, fascism. *American Anthropologist, 122*(3). https://www.americananthropologist.org/online-content/everything-is-permitted-trump-white-supremacy-fascism
Degerman, D., Flinders, M., & Johnson, M. T. (2020). In defence of fear: COVID-19, crises and democracy. *Critical Review of International Social and Political Philosophy.* https://doi.org/10.1080/13698230.2020.1834744
Dong, E., Du, H., & Gardner, L. (2020). An interactive web-based dashboard to track COVID-19 in real time. *The Lancet Infectious Diseases, 20*(5), P533–P534. https://doi.org/10.1016/S1473-3099(20)30120-1
Dorling, D. (2019). *Inequality and the 1%.* Verso.
El-Erian, M. (2021, 28 May). COVID vaccine crisis may be the last straw for the post-war economic consensus. *The Guardian.* https://www.theguardian.com/business/2021/may/28/covid-vaccine-crisis-may-be-the-last-straw-for-the-postwar-economic-consensus
Evans, G., & Mellon, J. (2019). Immigration, Euroscepticism, and the rise and fall of UKIP. *Party Politics, 25*(1), 76–87. https://doi.org/10.1177/1354068818816969
Foucault, M. (2003). *'Society must be defended': Lectures at the Collège de France, 1975–76.* Picador.
Gallagher, A., Davey, J., & Hart, M. (2020). *The genesis of a conspiracy theory: Key trends in QAnon activity since 2017.* Institute for Strategic Dialogue. https://www.isdglobal.org/wp-content/uploads/2020/07/The-Genesis-of-a-Conspiracy-Theory.pdf
Gardels, N., & Berggruen, N. (2019). *Renovating democracy: Governing in the age of globalization and digital capitalism.* University of California Press.
Gass, N. (2016, 4 April). Trump: 'The experts are terrible'. *Politico.* https://www.politico.com/blogs/2016-gop-primary-live-updates-and-results/2016/04/donald-trump-foreign-policy-experts-221528
Gates, B. (2015). The next outbreak? We're not ready. *TED.* https://www.ted.com/talks/bill_gates_the_next_outbreak_we_re_not_ready
Gerrard, J. (2021). The uneducated and the politics of knowing in 'post truth' times: Rancière, populism and in/equality. *Discourse: Studies in the Cultural Politics of Education, 42*(2), 155–169. https://doi.org/10.1080/01596306.2019.1595528
Giattino, C., Ritchie, H., Roser, M., Ortiz-Ospina, E., & Hasell, J. (2021, 11 August). *Excess mortality during the Coronavirus pandemic (COVID-19).* https://ourworldindata.org/excess-mortality-covid
Giroux, H. A. (2009). *Youth in a suspect society: Democracy or disposability?* Palgrave Macmillan.
Giroux, H. A. (2020, 7 April). The COVID-19 pandemic is exposing the plague of neoliberalism. *Truthout.* https://truthout.org/articles/the-covid-19-pandemic-is-exposing-the-plague-of-neoliberalism/
Goldberg, J. (2020, 17 November). Why Obama fears for our democracy. *The Atlantic.* https://www.theatlantic.com/ideas/archive/2020/11/why-obama-fears-for-our-democracy/617087/

Guterres, A. (2020, 23 April). We are all in this together: Human rights and COVID-19 response and recovery. *United Nations.* https://www.un.org/en/un-coronavirus-communications-team/we-are-all-together-human-rights-and-covid-19-response-and

Hopkin, J., & Blyth, M. (2020). Global Trumpism: Understanding anti-system politics in Western democracies. In B. Vormann & M. D. Weinman (Eds.), *The emergence of illiberalism* (pp. 101–123). Routledge.

Institute for Health Metrics and Evaluation. (2021, 13 May). *Estimation of excess mortality due to COVID-19.* http://www.healthdata.org/special-analysis/estimation-excess-mortality-due-covid-19-and-scalars-reported-covid-19-deaths

Laclau, E. (1977). *Politics and ideology in Marxist theory: Capitalism, fascism, populism.* New Left Books.

Laclau, E. (2005). *On populist reason.* Verso.

Lee, P. (2015). *Truth wars: The politics of climate change, military intervention and financial crisis.* Palgrave Macmillan.

Lévy, B.-H. (2020). *The virus in the age of madness.* Yale University Press.

Lipscy, P. Y. (2020). COVID-19 and the politics of crisis. *International Organization, 74,* E98–E127. https://doi.org/10.1017/S0020818320000375

Mance, H. (2016, 4 June). Britain has had enough of experts, says Gove. *Financial Times.* https://www.ft.com/content/3be49734-29cb-11e6-83e4-abc22d5d108c

McGowan, M. (2021, 16 February). How Australia became fertile ground for misinformation and QAnon. *The Guardian.* https://www.theguardian.com/australia-news/2021/feb/16/how-australia-became-fertile-ground-for-misinformation-and-qanon

McIntyre, L. (2018). *Post-truth.* The MIT Press.

Moffitt, B. (2015). How to perform crisis: A model for understanding the key role of crisis in contemporary populism. *Government and Opposition, 50*(2), 189–217. https://doi.org/10.1017/gov.2014.13

Moffitt, B. (2016). *The global rise of populism: Performance, political style and representation.* Stanford University Press.

Moffitt, B., & Tormey, S. (2014). Rethinking populism: Politics, mediatisation and political style. *Political Studies, 62*(2), 381–397. https://doi.org/10.1111/1467-9248.12032

Mouffe, C. (1993). *The return of the political.* Verso.

Mouffe, C. (1999). Deliberative democracy or agonistic pluralism? *Social Research, 66*(3), 745–758.

Mouffe, C. (2019). *For a left populism.* Verso.

Orwell, G. (1946). Politics and the English language. *Horizon, 13*(76), 252–265.

Osborne, P. (2021). *The assault on truth: Boris Johnson, Donald Trump and the emergence of a new moral barbarism.* Simon & Schuster.

O'Toole, F. (2020, 3 December). Democracy's afterlife: Trump, the GOP and the rise of zombie politics. *New York Review of Books.* https://www.nybooks.com/articles/2020/12/03/democracys-afterlife/

Pradhan, B., & Chaudhary, A. (2021, 22 July). COVID may have claimed as many as 5 million lives in India. *Bloomberg.* https://www.bloomberg.com/news/features/2021-07-21/covid-19-may-have-claimed-as-many-as-5-million-lives-in-india

Prati, G., & Mancini, A. D. (2021). The psychological impact of COVID-19 pandemic lockdowns: A review and meta-analysis of longitudinal studies and natural experiments. *Psychological Medicine, 51*(2), 201–211. https://doi.org/10.1017/S0033291721000015

Przeworski, A. (2019). *Crises of democracy.* Cambridge University Press.

Rancière, J. (2006). *Hatred of democracy.* Verso.

Rancière, J. (2010). *Dissensus: On politics and aesthetics.* Continuum.

Riddle, S., & Apple, M. W. (2019). *Re-imagining education for democracy.* Routledge.

Robinson, W. I. (2020, 17 June). Post-COVID economy may have more robots, fewer jobs and intensified surveillance. *Truthout*. https://truthout.org/articles/post-covid-economy-may-have-more-robots-fewer-jobs-and-intensified-surveillance/

Rosenvallon, P. (2017). *Counter-democracy: Politics in an age of distrust*. Cambridge University Press.

Sant, E. (2021). *Political education in times of populism: Towards a radical democratic education*. Palgrave Macmillan.

Sant, E., & Brown, T. (2020). The fantasy of the populist disease and the educational cure. *British Educational Research Journal*. https://doi.org/10.1002/berj.3666

Schostak, J., & Goodson, I. (2020). *Democracy, education and research: The struggle for public life*. Routledge.

Schwab, K., & Malleret, T. (2020). *COVID-19: The great reset*. Forum Publishing.

Srnicek, N., & Williams, A. (2016). *Inventing the future: Postcapitalism and a world without work*. Verso.

Temelkuran, E. (2019). *How to lose a country: The seven steps from democracy to dictatorship*. 4th Estate.

Tukekci, Z. (2020, 7 December). 'This must be your first': Acting as if Trump is trying to stage a coup is the best way to ensure he won't. *The Atlantic*. https://www.theatlantic.com/ideas/archive/2020/12/trumps-farcical-inept-and-deadly-serious-coup-attempt/617309/

Vaidhyanathan, S. (2018). *Antisocial media: How Facebook disconnects us and undermines democracy*. Oxford University Press.

Vasilopoulou, S. (2016). UK Euroscepticism and the Brexit referendum. *The Political Quarterly*, 87(2), 219–227. https://doi.org/10.1111/1467-923X.12258

Verma, R & Apple, M. W. (2021). Introduction: Understanding and interrupting hate. In R. Verma (Ed.), *Disrupting hate in education: Teacher activists, democracy and global pedagogies of interruption* (pp. 1–20). Routledge.

Vindegaard, N., & Benros, M. E. (2020). COVID-19 pandemic and mental health consequences: Systematic review of the current evidence. *Brain, Behavior, and Immunity*, 89, 531–542. https://doi.org/10.1016/j.bbi.2020.05.048

Wolf, M. (2020, 23 December). The fading light of liberal democracy. *Financial Times*. https://www.ft.com/content/47144c85-519a-4e25-9035-c5f8977cf6fd

Wong, J. C. (2020, 25 August). QAnon explained: The antisemitic conspiracy theory gaining traction around the world. *The Guardian*. https://www.theguardian.com/us-news/2020/aug/25/qanon-conspiracy-theory-explained-trump-what-is

Wu, H. (2020, 22 February). Sealed in: Chinese trapped at home by coronavirus feel the strain. *Reuters*. https://www.reuters.com/article/us-china-health-quarantine-idUSKCN20G0AY

Zakaria, F. (2020). *Ten lessons for a post-pandemic world*. W. W. Norton & Company.

Zembylas, M. (2020). The affective atmospheres of democratic education: Pedagogical and political implications for challenging right-wing populism. *Discourse: Studies in the Cultural Politics of Education*. https://doi.org/10.1080/01596306.2020.1858401

Žižek, S. (2020). *Pandemic! COVID-19 shakes the world*. OR Books.

4
A SELF-MADE CLIMATE CATASTROPHE

Introduction

> We have created a world that is always in overdrive. Human development in every sense has dramatically accelerated over the last two centuries, and that pace has quickened further in the last few decades. People are living longer, producing and consuming more, inhabiting larger spaces, consuming more energy, and generating more waste and greenhouse gas emissions.
>
> *(Zakaria, 2020, p. 18)*

Since the Industrial Revolution began in Europe and North America during the mid-eighteenth century with the emergence of the textile industry and the invention of the steam engine, human endeavours have had and continue to have profound impacts on natural ecological systems. The advent of mass production, electric power, digital communications technologies, automation and artificial intelligence has accelerated development and caused enormous disruption to the delicate ecological balance of our world. The effects of mechanisation, electrification, automation, digitalisation and globalisation are too numerous to list here; however, there is little doubt that the *Anthropocene* is an appropriate term to describe the magnitude of the effects of human activity on the lithosphere, biosphere, hydrosphere and atmosphere (Lewis & Maslin, 2015). Human activity has become a world-changing force, and it turns out, not necessarily for the better. While there have been positive outcomes in terms of quality of life, healthcare and economic prosperity over the past couple of centuries, such rewards have been unevenly distributed and enjoyed by a relative few, while many people continue to live in extreme situations of poverty, low-quality healthcare and face a future without clean water, clean air and clean food.

Despite the enormous advances in technology and human knowledge and understanding of the world, we find ourselves come to a point where the reckless indifference to the ecological harm caused by our 'progress' has begun to visibly take its toll. The science is clear—and has been for several decades now—that human activities are causing rapid climate change, alongside lasting harm to the environment, and have put into play a chain of events that will take decades, if not centuries, to mitigate and repair. The reliance on ecological systems for clean air, food and water cannot be taken for granted, yet it seems that is precisely what political and corporate leaders have done for decades now, against the evidence and against any sense of commitment to the future sustainability of life on the planet. Rather than deploying the significant technological, political and social tools already available, rich liberal–democratic societies have found themselves entirely unable, or unwilling to rise to the challenge. Decades of neoliberal policymaking have rendered the political and economic establishment as being entirely incapable of coping with the clear and present danger of the climate crisis. Instead, the political and economic response has been to ignore, prevaricate or shift the blame onto others, while the crisis continues to deepen. Taylor (2019) argued that 'with climate calamity on the near horizon, liberal democracies are in a bind. The dominant economic system constrains our relationship to the future, sacrificing humanity's well-being and the planet's resources on the altar of endless growth while enriching and empowering the global 1 percent' (p. 305). We must do something different before the calamity becomes entirely unavoidable.

There are significant similarities between the climate change crisis and the crisis of the COVID-19 global pandemic (see Chapter 3). Although one is playing out in ecological collapse and the other in virulent disease and death, both are exacerbated by the neoliberal policymaking of capitalist governments and the excesses of a globalised economic system intent on maximising extraction and burning of fossil fuels to feed a capitalist machine that requires increasing accelerated growth in production and consumption. Additionally, 'both have and will continue to interact in unpredictable and distinctive ways, ranging from the part played by diminished biodiversity in the behaviour of infectious diseases to the effect that COVID-19 might have on climate change, thus illustrating the perilously subtle balance and complex interactions between humankind and nature' (Schwab & Malleret, 2020, p. 95). In their analysis, Schwab and Malleret (2020) claimed that climate change and pandemics share five main attributes:

1. They are known systemic risks, which can rapidly escalate due to the interconnected nature of globalised economics and the movement of people and goods.
2. They are non-linear, with the capacity for threshold events (e.g., exponential transmission of a virus or climate chain reactions as systems break down).
3. They constantly shift and evolve, which makes the policy response necessarily adaptive.

4. They are global crises, which require global coordination.
5. They disproportionately affect those who are already marginalised and vulnerable.

However, one key difference between climate change and pandemics is in their time horizons, which Schwab and Malleret (2020) explained as the following:

> Pandemics are a quasi-instantaneous risk, whose imminence and danger are visible to all. An outbreak threatens our survival—as individuals or a species—and we therefore respond immediately and with determination when faced with the risk. By contrast, climate change and nature loss are gradual and cumulative, with effects that are discernible mostly in the medium and long term (and despite more and more climate related and 'exceptional' nature loss events, there are still significant numbers who remain unconvinced of the immediacy of the climate crisis). This crucial difference between the respective time-horizons of a pandemic and that of climate change and nature loss means that a pandemic risk requires immediate action that will be followed by a rapid result, while climate change and nature loss also require immediate action, but the result (or 'future reward', in the jargon of economists) will only follow with a certain time lag.
>
> *(Schwab & Malleret, 2020, p. 96)*

Further, while climate change is a real and present threat, the ongoing climate truth wars have caused substantial disruption, with the ideological battle continuing to rage between climate change scientists and activists against climate change sceptics (Lee, 2015), who have aligned with corporate and political actors in the ongoing quest to minimise, divert or downplay climate change action. In a country like Australia, the combined effects of conservative governments whose ministers move through a revolving door of government, political lobbying and fossil fuel corporation roles, alongside a media landscape dominated by Rupert Murdoch's NewsCorp, the discourse has been particularly toxic and damaging to any purposeful collective will to address the crisis. As one example of many, following a bitter and fear-fuelled election campaign in 2013, one of the first acts of the neoconservative and neoliberal Australian federal government, led by Prime Minister Tony Abbott, was to repeal the successful carbon tax that had been implemented by the former Labor government (Griffiths, 2014) and thus, completely undo the small gains made towards meaningful climate action at the federal level in Australia. Lee (2015) described such acts as enactments of a regime of climate truth. At this moment, there are sitting members of the Australian federal government who are vocal climate deniers, who have enormous followings on Facebook and spread their lies and disinformation without censure or erasure from either political or corporate leaders.

This chapter outlines some key features of the climate crisis, drawing on contemporary literature to consider the calamitous effects of anthropogenic climate change on natural and human systems. The crisis is both immediate and future-oriented, including global ecological collapse, the sixth major extinction event, mass displacement of human populations, increased global mean temperatures and cascading climate effects that have begun to produce a runaway, irreversible chain of events. However, at this moment, there are multiple points of hope and rupture within the inert and impotent political and economic apparatus, including the School Strike for Climate protests, Extinction Rebellion and other acts of resistance and fighting for a future, which are driven by young people. This chapter considers how these collective acts of resistance against political cowardice and inertia can provide important examples of democratic practice as a public pedagogy, which is both for, and of, young people. Mouffe (2019) claimed that 'it is impossible to envisage a project of radicalization of democracy in which the "ecological question" is not at the centre of the agenda' (p. 61). This chapter considers how this radicalisation of democracy through young people's commitment to ecological action can potentially open a new democratic horizon.

Hurtling Right Over the Climate Cliff

The first World Climate Conference was held at Geneva in 1979. Since that time, there have been hundreds of climate summits, countless scientific studies and multiple reports from the Intergovernmental Panel on Climate Change (the sixth assessment report is due for release in 2022). However, despite over 40 years of scientists clearly sounding the climate change alarm and warning political leaders, corporations and supranational organisations of the clear and present danger of climate change, 'we have generally conducted business as usual and have largely failed to address this predicament. The climate crisis has arrived and is accelerating faster than most scientists expected. It is more severe than anticipated, threatening natural ecosystems and the fate of humanity' (Ripple et al., 2020, pp. 8–9). Climate change, ecological collapse and environmental destruction are not the future outcomes of a reckless and indifferent capitalist mode of economic production, but are the here-and-now consequences, already causing widespread harm and devastation for people, animals and the natural systems in which we live and upon which we rely for our survival as a species.

The Intergovernmental Panel on Climate Change devised the 'reasons for concern' framework to determine levels of climate risk and inform policymakers in their judgements. The tool provides broad analyses of risks to unique and threatened systems, extreme weather events, distribution and aggregation of impacts, and large-scale singular events. Without rapid reductions in emissions, there is a very high risk of widespread and potentially irreversible global impacts during the twenty-first century (O'Neill et al., 2017). Already, there has been a doubling in the global population exposed to extreme weather events such as cyclones, flooding, wildfires, drought and heatwaves, with modelling suggesting that this figure will increase to fivefold with 2°C warming (Lange et al., 2020).

The climate emergency is here and wishful thinking on the part of governments and corporations will not make it otherwise (Cox, 2020). The natural systems that support our lives and livelihoods have been disrupted and destabilised to the point of no return, and only urgent and radical action is going to be able to ensure a livable century for the people, plants and animals on this planet. The Paris Agreement to keep warming to 1.5°C above the pre-industrial average is almost certainly doomed to fail, and indeed, 'we are already experiencing unprecedented damage from heat waves, droughts, fires and cyclones, and the Earth's climate system is now changing so rapidly that science is struggling to keep up, and this is occurring at a rising global temperature of about 1.1°C' (Flannery, 2020, p. 50). However, we are facing a century in which the possibility of 4°C warming is real, which would threaten the world's water supply, result in a massive extinction event and widespread ecological collapse, as well as making many coastal cities and deltas on which some of the largest cities have been built completely uninhabitable. This sounds like the stuff of dystopian future fiction, yet it is the future that awaits humanity as it walks (some blindly, some wilfully) into the future unprepared for the existential crisis. For some, the existential crisis is already here.

Bradshaw et al. (2021) claimed that the challenges of climate change continue to be misunderstood and underestimated, which increases the likelihood of irreversible damage. They argued that the challenges include rapid biodiversity loss, the beginnings of the sixth mass extinction event, overconsumption, climate disruption, population displacement and political impotence (Bradshaw et al., 2021). Together, these challenges present a bleak picture of the medium-term future of humanity over the twenty-first century, although with the political will, technological innovation and economic drive, perhaps societies can rise to meet the challenge. As it currently stands, the neoliberal policies of most developed liberal democracies continue to perpetuate Keynesian solutions, which 'are the motors of environmental destruction' (Mouffe, 2019, p. 52). Instead of taking decisive action to decarbonise and prevent further emissions, the prevarication of governments in aiding and abetting the climate vandalism of corporate oligarchs has ensured that the first decades of the twenty-first century have been largely wasted on climate inaction, which has set in motion a series of climate feedback loops (Steffen et al., 2018).

Climate feedback loops have the potential to induce a 'hothouse' effect, in which runaway temperature increases will cause catastrophic disruption to ecosystems. The Earth System—biosphere, climate and human societies—requires rapid decarbonisation, new economic and governance settings on a global and local scale, plus fundamental changes to behaviours and social values to avoid a 'hothouse' Earth, which would be likely irreversible and calamitous (Steffen et al., 2018). The threat of climate feedback loops and tipping points is too great to ignore, as evidence grows of the interconnected nature of different biophysical systems, which will lead to devastating short- and long-term effects (Lenton et al., 2019). For example, the interconnected, globalised food system is highly vulnerable to climate change, with significant threats to wheat, soybean and maize crops with 1.5°C warming, and widespread crop failure over 2°C warming (Gaupp et al., 2019). Further, 37 per cent of heat-related deaths globally between 1991 and 2018 were attributed to climate change, with mortality increasing over the period (Vicedo-Cabrera et al., 2021). There is no doubt that a warming planet poses immediate and longer-term danger to the sustainability of life on Earth. Radical climate action is urgently required, in the order of global emissions reductions of at least 7.6 per cent per year over the next decade (Flannery, 2020), which is well outside the scope of current climate policymaking by governments around the globe.

The current settings of publicly stating the aim of net zero emissions by 2050, while continuing to subsidise and support fossil fuel extraction and usage is a key theme of countries like the US and Australia. The fossil fuel lobby remains powerful even though it is facing a steep decline in economic and political influence over the coming years. It is politically convenient to claim to certain emission reduction targets, of which 'net zero by 2050' is a favourite because it pushes back the problem of addressing the climate crisis and makes it a problem for someone else, later on. Of course, those who are most going to suffer the consequences of this prevarication, gaslighting and denialism are the young people in our schools and kindergartens, and those young people yet to come. The net zero discourse is not simply politically convenient for political leaders; it is also dangerous because:

> Current net zero policies will not keep warming to within 1.5°C because they were never intended to. They were and still are driven by a need to protect business as usual, not the climate. If we want to keep people safe then large and sustained cuts to carbon emissions need to happen now. That is the very simple acid test that must be applied to all climate policies. The time for wishful thinking is over.
>
> *(Dyke et al., 2021, np)*

The time for wishful thinking is indeed over. However, it seems that many of our political, social and economic institutions and those who control them are either disinterested or malignantly opposed to meaningful climate action. The hold of capitalist hegemony over the political and social apparatus remains strong, despite the clear evidence that the longer we delay in taking radical action to mitigate the worst effects of climate change, the worse it will get. It seems that Schostak and Goodson (2020) were correct when they claimed that 'the demand for cheap goods and services is more effective than the demand for freedom, equality and a world safe for all' (p. 137). The profit motive, combined with a weakened public, has ensured a long period of immobility and indecision. This has been helped by the atomisation of individuals and the hollowing out of democratic engagement. We need a public force that is capable of tackling the enormous task ahead, and which is unafraid of dismantling the corporate oligarchy and refashioning the economic, political and social tools for a more sustainable democratic future. We face an era of runaway climate change, massive inequality and political inertia (Monbiot, 2016), which must be resisted. A new democratic horizon must be formed, and the best hope is with young people taking radical collective democratic action, inside and outside of schools and other sites of learning.

Importantly, Seitzinger et al. (2012) argued for a more thoughtful approach to planetary stewardship, which accounts for the interconnected nature of ecosystems and human political and economic systems, the increasing effects of urbanisation and limited resources, and how the future could be socially, economically and environmentally sustainable. Further, Deese (2019) contended that the challenge of climate change requires forms of democracy that move beyond traditional Westphalian system of separate, competing nation states who vie for ever-dwindling resources and seek to accumulate economic, political and cultural power. Instead, more localised and globalised forms of democratic accountability are required, which move across societies in multiple ways and at multiple levels, including in education, work and civic life. Similarly, Taylor (2019) claimed that we need more socialist economic systems that connect to democratic modes of investment, which drive ecological sustainability and publicly available infrastructure in support of a zero-carbon society. Of course, 'there's no assurance that ecological sustainability will be guaranteed under a more socialist system, but subordinating our collective survival to the short-term imperatives of the market means we don't stand a chance' (Taylor, 2019, p. 303). There is no doubt that:

> We live in a world where climate change threatens our economies, our land and our lives. The seas are rising, largely unnoticed; birds, frogs and other animals are silently disappearing. The summers are getting warmer and drier. We have sleepwalked deep into the world that exists just seconds before the climate clock strikes a catastrophic midnight.
> *(Flannery, 2020, p. 179)*

Those in charge of our political and economic institutions have absolutely failed in their responsibility to lead society towards a more sustainable future, placing us instead on a path towards certain calamity without radical and immediate action. Instead, Klein (2014) argued that what is needed is a different kind of shock doctrine, in which climate change prompts a *People's Shock* from below. 'As part of the project of getting our emissions down to the levels many scientists recommend, we once again have the chance to advance policies that dramatically improve lives, close the gap between rich and poor, create huge numbers of good jobs, and reinvigorate democracy from the ground up' (Klein, 2014, p. 19). However, it remains to be seen whether the political will can be spurred to action. It may already be too late, which only increases the need for more radical forms of democratic engagement, led by young people and in the name of a future for young people, who are inheriting a world that will soon become unliveable without drastic action now.

Civil Disobedience and a Public Pedagogy of Resistance

Kaukko et al. (2021) posed the paradox of education being both part of the problem and the possible solution. Education, and schooling in particular, has long reinforced the process of social, cultural and economic production within societies. The practices of education have helped to shape the human world with all its great challenges. However, a more sustainable and caring future is possible if we consider the ways in which we can change our practices, including our educational practices, to ensure we get there. There are lessons to be learned from acts of political resistance and civil disobedience, through which schools and other sites of learning can be reclaimed as democratic public spaces (Brady, 2006).

As one possible response to the paradox of schooling as a problem and solution, Giroux (2003, 2004, 2005, 2010) has argued extensively for a *public pedagogy* that resists the political project of neoliberalism and capitalism to reclaim the creative and critical spaces for engagement with public cultures and institutions. His work has been highly influential with cultural studies and critical studies in education, although perhaps at its heart is an unwavering commitment to the public good through critical engagement with pedagogy in all its forms, including the pedagogy of resistance and civil disobedience. Importantly, public pedagogy supports and extends an inclusive radical democracy that works directly against the divisive and shallow market democracy enabled by neoliberal politics in the interest of corporate oligarchs. Further, Giroux (2005) claimed that:

> We need a new understanding of how culture works as a form of public pedagogy, how pedagogy works as a moral and political practice, how agency is organized through pedagogical relations, how individuals can be educated to make authority responsive, how politics can make the workings of power visible and accountable, and how hope can be reclaimed in dark times through new forms of pedagogical praxis, global protests, and collective resistance.
>
> *(p. 85)*

Acts of civil disobedience and resistance are generally cast as being antisocial and destabilising acts of aggression against the state. However, 'when we do not live in a functioning democracy but hope to create one, we may find that it is our democratic duty to break the laws if at least some of them are unjust. We call this refusal of consent civil disobedience' (Taylor, 2019, p. 159). Importantly, Mouffe (1999) argued that the aim is not to eliminate power through anarchic destabilisation, but to reconstitute politics and institutions to support forms of power that are more compatible with democratic values. The erosion of democratic modes and practices through globalisation, neoliberalism and the increasing concentration of wealth and power in the hands of a few (Brown, 2011) has made it impossible for people to have power and a meaningful voice within contemporary political discourses, without seeking to subvert and reclaim political spaces. Acts of civil disobedience and the public pedagogy of resistance are powerful markers of reclaiming these spaces.

The project of radical democratisation through public acts of resistance is multi-dimensional, multi-layered and counter-capitalist, which requires counter-hegemonic ideals that push back against the dominant discourses of social and political recognition (Amsler, 2015). New democratic frontiers present an existential threat to the one per cent who seek to maintain and extend their wealth, power and privilege (Dorling, 2019). Therefore, radical democratisation is not something that is simply resisted by the powerful, but actively framed as a threat to the very existence of society itself. Writing about the Occupy movement, Amsler (2015) suggested that radical democracy requires 'sensibilities that are understood to be oppositional in neoliberal societies: dissensus, a radical openness to difference and dialogue, deep and reflexive criticality, the decentring and tearing away of certainties, a commitment to long-term transformation, and a passion for permanent possibility' (p. 198). It is through productive difference, affirmative and active engagement with each other that a democratic impulse can be nurtured and sustained.

The Occupy movement had its beginnings in the Arab Spring, which was a series of protests and anti-government rebellions that swept across Tunisia, Egypt, Yemen, Syria and Libya from December 2010. While there were different groups and political aims that arose during the Occupy movement, it was a loose international progressive movement that sought to address gross social and economic inequalities, neoliberal and austerity economics, and to ignite a revolution of 'real democracy' in response to the weakened forms under capitalism. Amsler (2015) argued that 'long before the Occupy movement began, people knew that capitalism was out of control and that crisis and inequality were calculated effects of the "upward distribution" of wealth and power rather than hapless consequences of disarticulated policies' (p. 43). Szolucha (2016) claimed that liberty and equality are necessary for democracy to work, although the liberal representative model under capitalism produced a version of individual liberty that came at the expense of social equality, public good and social inclusion. When the wave of social discontent broke—first in the Arab world against corruption and authoritarian tyranny, then in the liberal–democratic heartland of globalised capitalism—the outpouring of collective desire for democratic change was global. For example, Szolucha (2016) argued that:

> It was no coincidence that the biggest economic crisis in decades was in fact a twin crisis; the financial crisis coincided with a crisis of democracy. It was also not by chance that a host of new pro-democratic social movements sprang up in response to this crisis. Throughout its modern history, democracy has developed in tandem with capitalism on the one hand, and popular politics and protest on the other. It was, therefore, inevitable that

democracy would be implicated in the current crisis both as its culprit and as a potential force that could bring about more egalitarian forms of social and political life.

(p. 19)

The Occupy movement exposed the limitations of contemporary representative democracy as a thin form of democratic engagement, and instead brought direct, deliberative and participatory democracy to the centre. The Occupy movement sought societal change through the micropolitics of direct democracy, which in the end, was the source of its eventual inward collapse as a social and political movement, given the scale and scope of the project in reshaping global capital. However, there are salient lessons to be gained from the Occupy movement, which speak to contemporary social and political movements, including those that seek a commitment to ecological sustainability such as the School Strikes for Climate and Extinction Rebellion.

First, the Occupy movement demonstrated that widespread civil disobedience and public resistance to the hegemony of the corporate oligarchy and political class can make a difference when it is done at scale and with a collective will that is impossible to ignore. Second, the Occupy movement challenged non-representation and called for more inclusive participatory forms of democratic engagement through deliberative and direct democratic action. Finally, the Occupy movement demonstrated that the 99 per cent wield enormous power, and have the capacity to enact radical democratic change. As Amsler (2015) argued, 'those who know how social worlds are *made* have always understood that they can be *remade*; that if capitalism is *done* then economic life can be done *differently*; that if subjectivities are *performed* we can become *otherwise*' (p. 46). The Occupy movement showed us that we can become otherwise and formed a public pedagogy in the process.

A few years after the Occupy movement had dissipated, the worldwide 2017 Women's March following Trump's inauguration as US President was claimed to be the largest day of civil protest in the US, with up to 4.6 million protesters demonstrating against the sexism and misogyny perpetrated and represented by an openly racist and misogynist Trump (Broomfield, 2017). Writing on the power of public resistance and deliberative democracy as represented by the Women's March and the Occupy movement, Rowe and Gerrard (2019) claimed that 'the spectacular performative act of gathering on the street retains a certain amount of power to enact a collective popular politics and labouring to *represent*. This politics can, of course, take many forms, but at its heart it has a democratic impulse' (p. 29). They provided the caveat, channelling Butler (2016), that when 'the people' strive to represent, there is always an outside because 'the people' can never truly be fully representative, although more inclusive aims towards collective action are the desired end of such actions.

For young people, climate change presents a clear and present danger to their lives and livelihoods over the coming decades. There is substantial evidence that young people are feeling anxious about their future under catastrophic climate change (Clayton, 2020), with themes of climate anxiety permeating through popular culture (McGinn, 2019). Wu et al. (2020) suggested that young people are at a high risk to develop new psychological conditions or worsen existing mental illness due to climate anxiety because 'they are at a crucial point in their physical and psychological development, when enhanced vulnerability to the effects of stress and everyday anxiety elevate their risk of developing depression, anxiety, and substance use disorders' (p. 435). It is little wonder that the inaction of governments, business and civic leaders has left young people feeling unseen, unheard and unaccounted for. As a result, through courageous acts of civil disobedience and resistance, young people have reclaimed their democratic impulse to demand change.

Over a million school students from more than 150 countries joined in the global climate strikes in September 2019 (Taylor et al., 2019). The response from Australian federal politicians, including the acting prime minister, was to argue that school students should have protested on the weekend rather than skipping school because of its disruption to their schooling (O'Brien & Baker, 2019). Similarly, teachers in the UK were barred from demonstrating and encouraged to penalise students for being absent from school (Busby, 2019). Since the initial marches began in 2019, inspired by youth climate activists such as Greta Thunberg, Isra Hirsi, Alexandria Villaseñor, Xiye Bastida, Vic Barrett and Katie Eder (Neela-Stock, 2019), the movement has grown to a worldwide coalition of students and others, who demand climate justice.

Swarbrick (2021) argued that the School Strike for Climate is 'the purest form of politics there is: People power. ... These kids aren't asking for power. They are making it out of nothing, with tools and imagination beyond what can be taken for granted. Discomfort is their norm. It shouldn't come as a surprise to us when they win' (np). The demands of young people for climate justice are intimately woven through with a radical democratic praxis that has at its heart a commitment to the inclusive collective well-being and future of people and other animals and ecosystems. Climate justice will require the inversion of economic and political structures that perpetuate environmental harm and continue to precipitate and accelerate ecological collapse, species loss and the destructive reliance on the extraction and burning of fossil fuels in the name of globalised capital's lust for endless growth and profit for shareholders.

Further, Mattheis (2020) suggested that the youth climate movement engages in acts of principled civil disobedience by young people who are excluded from the political and economic spheres of social influence. As such, the power available to them is the power which they create themselves through disruption, resistance and disobedience. As 16-year-old Swedish climate activist, Greta Thunberg, declared at the 2019 climate protests, 'We have only been born into this world; we are going to have to live with this crisis our whole lives. So will our children and grandchildren and coming generations. We are not going to accept this. We are striking because we want a future' (Westbrook & Fraser, 2019, np).

The demands of young people to be heard and counted have confronted and confounded political leaders, who have either ignored, attempted to placate or derided and attempted to reduce the activism of students as youthful excess and delinquency. Mayes and Hartup (2021, 2022) argued that the media representations and institutional responses to the youth climate protests have attempted to portray the students as ignorant zealots, anxious pawns, rebellious truants and, in relatively few instances, extraordinary heroes. The response of education departments, school principals and politicians was to admire the 'passion' of the young activists, while also sternly reminding them that their education should not suffer as a result. In response to these portrayals of concerned adults wishing for young people to be able to express themselves while still remaining excluded from political forms of power, young activists responded by arguing that:

> This movement had to happen, we didn't have a choice. We knew there was a climate crisis. Not just because forests in Sweden or in the US had been on fire; because of alternating floods and drought in Germany and Australia; because of the collapse of alpine faces due to melting permafrost and other climate changes. We knew, because everything we read and watched screamed out to us that something was very wrong. … We have watched as politicians fumble, playing a political game rather than facing the facts that the solutions we need cannot be found within the current system. They don't want to face the facts—we need to change the system if we are to try to act on the climate crisis. This movement had to happen, we didn't have a choice. The vast majority of climate strikers taking action today aren't allowed to vote. Imagine for a second what that feels like. Despite watching the climate crisis unfold, despite knowing the facts, we aren't allowed to have a say in who makes the decisions about climate change. And then ask yourself this: wouldn't you go on strike too, if you thought doing so could help protect your own future?
>
> *(Thunberg et al., 2019, np)*

There are many youth-led and youth-focused organisations that are committed to building local and global movements for climate justice. Some key Australian examples include the Australian Youth Climate Coalition and the Seed Indigenous Youth Climate Network. On their website, Seed claim that climate change is an environmental and social justice issue, which disproportionately affects marginalised communities, including First Nations peoples, communities of colour, people living in poverty, women and youth. Seed founder and National Director, Amelia Telford, argued that 'we need to approach social movements and build the power of the people in a way that doesn't perpetuate the same systems that have got us here' (Ward, 2020, np).

Importantly, the climate crisis is not experienced equally by all young people. Those in capitalised liberal–democratic societies already enjoy comparative wealth and advantage, which enables them to have the chance to 'take a risk' and protest against the injustices of political and economic systems that perpetuate the climate crisis. Taking time off school to march is a privilege that not all young people can share. For example, millions of young people either have no access to school or experience routine school absences due to displacement, violence, famine, religious and cultural persecution or climate-related reasons such as extreme weather events and failed harvests, through which the entrenched geographical, economic, social and generational disadvantage is heightened and extended by the climate crisis (Walker, 2020).

Recently, promising gains have been made through the climate activism of young people and the global movement for climate justice. For example, in May 2021, a Dutch court ordered that Royal Dutch Shell—a large multinational fossil fuel company worth approximately US $160 billion—reduce its greenhouse gas emissions by 45 per cent by 2030 (Bousso et al., 2021), opening the way for legal action against other multinational energy companies. Similarly, investor pressure has increased on large oil companies, with Exxon Mobil and Chevron being forced to adopt stricter reduction targets (Lannin, 2021). Perhaps most astonishingly, Australian Federal Court Justice Mordecai Bromberg found that the federal government, specifically the Environment Minister, has a duty of care to children to not act in a way that causes future harm through climate change (Morton, 2021). The class action was launched in 2020 to prevent an expansion of a coal mine by eight young Australian climate activists on behalf of children around the globe (Young, 2020). Additionally, in the wake of an explosion and fire that resulted in a catastrophic turbine failure at a Queensland coal-fired power station, the state government announced that it was bringing forward plans for additional renewable energy projects, including large-scale battery storage, hydroelectric and solar power generation (Nothling, 2021).

These public and collective acts of civil disobedience and resistance against the capitalist oligarchs and neoliberal policymakers by young people are a radical form of public pedagogy, which seeks to reclaim and reshape democratic practices in a sustainable and inclusive way. Working as a dynamic counterbalance to more formal sites of education, such as schools, youth-led social movements offer up the opportunity for young people to learn from themselves and each other, and perhaps as importantly, teach adults how to meaningfully engage with the world and its problems in a compelling and collaborative manner, in what Biswas and Mattheis (2021) described as a *childist* pedagogy. For example, the student climate strikes are an important opportunity for young people to invert the political and social power structures, to demonstrate the potential for intergenerational collaboration and action, and to demonstrate how young people are already in the process of political engagement, rather than being not-yet-formed citizens-in-waiting who must wait until they finish school before becoming part of society.

The Kids Will Be Alright

> The future of our species in the age of climate change will depend on how we answer two basic questions. First, are we capable of governing ourselves? Second, are we capable of using the fire that technology has put into our hands without burning up the world? The first question concerns our relationship to each other, while the second question concerns our relationship to nature. If there was ever a time when the two questions could be answered separately, that time has long since passed. As it stands now, these questions must be faced together, and the answer will be the same for both. If the answer to these questions is no, it will be a definitive no, settled once and for all time. This negative result will most likely entail a collapse of the world's major democracies and the ecologically stable systems on which they depend. If the answer to these questions is yes, it will always be a provisional yes, as when we say 'so far, so good' and keep a wary eye on the future.
>
> (Deese, 2019, p. 7)

The climate crisis represents an existential threat and the warnings from scientists and climate activists around the world are entirely unambiguous. There is no further room for prevarication, hesitation or bastard acts of political and economic skulduggery, such as the greenwashing attempts currently underway by large corporations and governments seeking to rebadge themselves as enthusiastic supporters of a net zero future. However, we cannot wait for the future to take the drastic action required, and young people understand this much more clearly than the adults who are in charge of the political and economic systems that could and should be acting with urgency. Every day counts and the next few years present us with our last chance to make meaningful change before it is too late (Flannery, 2020).

Young people have led the charge for change and demonstrated the power of collective action, which can enable the commitment to climate justice and new forms of solidarity that have ecological sustainability at their heart. The active engagement with a public pedagogy and vigorous participatory democracy go together, in which young people are able to engage in productive solutions and agitate for democratic processes and actions in response to the clear and present danger of climate change. Importantly, such actions are driven by hope, which is an essential part of the belief that the future can be different. As Amsler (2015) argued, 'we want to believe that we can refuse the futures given us and determine our own; that we can tend to and heal the pains of the present; and that we can experience joy, comfort and liberation in everyday life' (p. 55). The direct action of young climate activists is as much an expression of hope, solidarity and love as it is disobedience and a refusal to accept the status quo from governments and corporations that are clearly unwilling and unable to take the action needed to decarbonise and ensure a cleaner, greener and more sustainable future.

Climate change has brought contemporary civilisation to the limits of unchecked growth and ecological vandalism in the name of economic prosperity (for the few), while leaving the majority of people living in unacceptable conditions, including poor air and water quality, over-production and extraction resulting in degraded environments, food quality and shortages, leading to malnutrition, all while being increasingly exposed to climate change fuelled extreme weather events. We need to find new ways of living within the world, which are socially, politically, environmentally, economically and culturally sustainable. A more ecologically minded democracy is required, which is committed to environmental justice (Fischer, 2017). It will not be enough to deploy new technologies and scientific solutions to tackle the challenges of climate change. A radical rethinking of the structures and institutions that have enabled planetary vandalism and destruction to proceed apace for decades is essential, and this must come through acts of localised and globalised democracy, through collective and collaborative experimentation in living in ways that nurture and extend our relationships with the world, rather than seeing it as a set of resources to be exploited for wealth and personal gain.

It is clear that alternative forms of localised democratic governance are required to deepen the bonds with human and natural systems, through an emphasis on democratic environmental participation to create a global environmental democracy (Fischer, 2017) that engages all people, but especially those who have been marginalised and left at the fringes—the young, First Nations and communities of colour, migrants and refugees, as well as people living in precarity and poverty—to engage in direct action and activism to build futures for their communities. The climate crisis presents an opening for more engaged forms of democratic participation to be possible, but first the barriers to inclusion must be removed, and the structures of capitalism and neoliberal policymaking must be recast in the interests of the 99 per cent rather than the 1 per cent.

In addition to localised forms of democratic governance, Deese (2019) claimed that climate change will require new models of international governance, with a view to ecologically sustainable forms of democratic engagement and participation on a global scale. However, 'there are two broad questions about government facing the human race in the Anthropocene. The first is, can we govern nature? The second is, can we govern ourselves? The most probable answer to the first of these questions, in spite of our advances in technology, is no. The only honest answer to the second question is maybe' (Deese, 2019, p. 133). While there are many problems with supranational organisations like the United Nations, World Bank, World Health Organization and International Monetary Fund—given that they were formed and continue to operate within neoliberal policy rationalities—there is an important role for global institutions alongside more localised forms of democracy to ensure that young people have a future worth saving.

Of course, engagement in democracy requires that sovereignty is democratised in the interests of those who are currently least advantaged by the political and economic systems and structures that govern people's lives. Aslam (2017) argued for active citizenship and popular legislative power as being necessary first steps to breaking the cycle of acquiescence and domination that have characterised the passive relationship of neoliberal capitalist consumer-subjects to state power. The youth climate strikes are one example of democratising sovereignty and reclaiming political power in the pursuit of more sustainable modes of economic and political life.

Young people have clearly articulated themselves as having strong agency and political subjectivities, although they remain excluded from representative democratic participation and cannot yet vote in elections and the like. However, as Biesta (2011) argued, there are important lessons in democratic citizenship that young people can both experience as learners and offer to society in their participatory engagement in democratic action within schools and other institutions, as well as through acts of civil disobedience and resistance. This is because:

> Democratic politics does not require a particular kind of political subjectivity in order for it to be possible. The political subject, the agent of democratic politics, arises in and with democratic action itself. In its shortest form: the political subject is not so much the producer of consensus as that it is the 'product' of dissensus. It is not, therefore, that education needs to make individuals ready for democratic politics; it is rather that through engagement in democratic politics political subjectivity is engendered. By turning the relationship between political subjectivity and democratic politics on its head, Rancière shifts education from its traditional place as the 'producer' of political subjectivities.
>
> *(Biesta, 2011, p. 95)*

This brings to mind Dewey's (1899) claim that school is not a site of preparation for life or a place where lessons are learned separate from the world, but a site of active engagement and participation in community life, through which the democratic spirit can be fostered and extended. Schools are important community hubs and offer the opportunity to connect young people, educators, parents and other community members in meaningful encounters that enable democratic participation and the building of a community that engages in constructive debates about how society should be structured to best support its people and the places in which they live (Giroux, 2016), rather than a site of testing, ranking and sorting young people according to academic achievement or social and cultural position.

However, it is clear that 'questions about the social, economic and cultural purposes of education have always been the subject of contentious political debate' (Carr & Hartnett, 1996, p. 17). Neoconservatives, religious fundamentalists and neoliberal proponents have long viewed schools as something to be tightly controlled and carefully limited to sites for preparing the vast majority of young people to be compliant consumers and fodder for the globalised and precarious workforce, while a select few (i.e., those children of the elite) are provided with a privileged classical liberal education in preparation for their future roles as corporate and political leaders. McLaren and Farahmandpur (2005) claimed that 'capitalist schooling participates in the production, distribution, and circulation of knowledge and skills necessary for reproducing the social division of labor and hence capitalist relations of exploitation' (pp. 50–51). It brings to mind Plato's (2007) argument for the specialised education of *Philosopher-Kings*, who are to be kept separate from the education of the general population in preparation for their role as the ruling class. Unsurprising, when considering that Plato argued against Athenian democracy as enabling tyranny of the mob, through which base impulses of the masses drove decision-making rather than a guided commitment to the common good. However, Schostak (2019) has warned against such an approach as education that serves the interests of the powerful:

> If education is employed to privilege the development of the powers and interests of some over others, it becomes reduced to a form of engineering to fit the interests of the powerful rather than the interests of all. Consequently, to avoid the abuse of power by one or more against others and promote social justice, I argue that discourses of equality and radical inclusion are co-extensive with democracy, co-operation and education in the production of a society of equals.
>
> (p. 1104)

The climate crisis demands more radically inclusive forms of education and democratic practice because the scope and scale of the challenges arising from ecological collapse require new ways of thinking and working together on collaborative solutions for highly complex problems. A radical democratic approach must 'articulate the ecological and social questions. It is necessary to imagine a new synthesis between key aspects of the democratic and socialist traditions around a new model of development' (Mouffe, 2019, p. 52). It is possible that the climate crisis will be a catalyst for fundamental and productive societal change, through the revitalisation of economic systems and reshaping production and consumption processes, reviving public spaces and institutions, reclaiming the commons and reworlding the human environments to be more inclusive and sustaining for all. Klein (2014) argued that a radical shift in our thinking and practices is required to address gross inequality and reset the balance in favour of ecological sustainability and healthy lives. Klein (2014) extended the argument to call for a broad-based network of local and global, grassroots movements that are 'driven by a desire for a deeper form of democracy, one that provides communities with real control over those resources that are most critical to collective survival—the health of the water, air, and soil. In the process, these place-based stands are stopping real climate crimes in progress' (p. 302).

Social movements, collectivism and grassroots organisations that engage directly with young people in meaningful and democratic ways offer not only possible solutions to the climate crisis but also important lessons in the democratisation of life generally. There is enormous power in collective and collaborative organisation, including acts of disobedience and resistance such as marches, protests, boycotts, strikes, riots and occupations. As Taylor (2019) argued, the ecological catastrophe requires the radical reshaping of economies and modes of production and consumption, and while our governments and multinational corporations have proven themselves to be wholly inadequate to the enormity of the task, young people have shown the way. However, young people should not be left to bear the burdens of climate justice alone, but rather need the support and engagement of broader communities, which are active and resilient in the face of opposition from the elites who seek to retain the status quo. On the participatory culture of active and engaged communities, Monbiot (2018) argued that the commitment to public life supports more just and inclusive politics, demonstrating a clear sense of civic responsibility and articulation of values and principles of sustainability, participation and common ground. Indeed, 'a flourishing community stimulates our innate urge to cooperate. It helps immunise us against extremism and demagoguery, and it turns democracy into a daily habit. Community is the place from which a new politics begins to grow' (Monbiot, 2018, p. 132).

As important community sites of public encounter and engagement with cultural and social diversity and difference, schools have the opportunity to be part of a project of radical democratisation rather than simply acting as producers of human capital or reinscribing the social and cultural renderings upon young people. A creative and critical citizenry requires a schooling that is committed to the principles of radical equality and principled resistance against the forms of oppression and tyranny that come with living in a time of globalised capitalist neoliberalism, when education policy is rendered as a function of market-based economics and the production of education consumers. The ideological apparatus of schooling itself needs to be reformed in the interests of those who are least advantaged by the present system, to better support young people in becoming capable and creative collaborators on solving the pressing issues facing them, not the least of which is the climate crisis and impending ecological collapse over the coming years and decades.

Business as usual simply won't suffice for schooling, so teachers, school leaders, parents and carers, and other community members will need to engage with young people in more democratic and inclusive ways to ensure that they are given the chance to not simply survive, but to thrive. The pedagogical encounters and the curriculum within schools must support the development of a more critical democracy, which links the struggles of public life to the lived realities, hopes and dreams of young people, rather than organising school curriculum and pedagogy based on the interests of the ruling class. As Aronowitz and Giroux (1991) argued 20 years ago, the project of schooling must be political and pedagogical, combining a democratic public philosophy with radical acts of resistance. It seems that 'if we want a creative citizenry that is capable of constituting itself as a democratic public sphere, then curriculum and school organizations must address the imaginary, and refrain from finding techniques to displace it by fear to the prevailing order' (Aronowitz & Giroux, 1987, p. 20). As intellectual workers, teachers have an important role to play in helping young people to be critical and creative agents of democratic change for a more inclusive, caring and sustainable society. The future of our planet and human survival depends upon it.

References

Amsler, S. S. (2015). *The education of radical democracy*. Routledge.
Aronowitz, S., & Giroux, H. (1987). *Education under siege: The conservative, liberal and radical debate over schooling*. Routledge & Keegan Paul Ltd.
Aronowitz, S., & Giroux, H. (1991). *Postmodern education: Politics, culture and social criticism*. University of Minnesota Press.
Aslam, A. (2017). *Ordinary democracy: Sovereignty and citizenship beyond the neoliberal impasse*. Oxford University Press.
Biesta, G. (2011). *Learning democracy in school and society: Education, lifelong learning, and the politics of citizenship*. Sense Publishers.
Biswas, T., & Mattheis, N. (2021). Strikingly educational: A childist perspective on children's civil disobedience for climate justice. *Educational Philosophy and Theory*. https://doi.org/10.1080/00131857.2021.1880390
Bousso, R., Meijer, B., & Nasralla, S. (2021, 26 May). Shell ordered to deepen carbon cuts in landmark Dutch climate case. *Reuters*. https://www.reuters.com/business/sustainable-business/dutch-court-orders-shell-set-tougher-climate-targets-2021-05-26/
Bradshaw, C. J. A., Ehrlich, P. R., Beattie, A., Ceballos, G., Crist, E., Diamond, J., Dirzo, R., Ehrlich, A. H., Harte, J., Harte, M. E., Pyke, G., Raven, P. H., Ripple, W. J., Saltré, F., Turnbull, C., Wackernagel, M., & Blumstein, D. T. (2021). Understanding the challenges of avoiding a ghastly future. *Frontiers in Conservation Science*. https://doi.org/10.3389/fcosc.2020.615419
Brady, J. F. (2006). Public pedagogy and educational leadership: Politically engaged scholarly communities and possibilities for critical engagement. *Journal of Curriculum & Pedagogy*, 3(1), 57–60. https://doi.org/10.1080/15505170.2006.10411575
Broomfield, M. (2017, 23 January). Women's March against Donald Trump is the largest day of protests in US history, say political scientists. *The Independent*. https://www.independent.co.uk/news/world/americas/womens-march-anti-donald-trump-womens-rights-largest-protest-demonstration-us-history-political-scientists-a7541081.html
Brown, W. (2011). 'We are all democrats now…'. In G. Agamben, A. Badiou, D. Bensaïd, W. Brown, J.-L. Nancy, J. Rancière, K. Ross, & S. Žižek (Eds.), *Democracy in what state?* (pp. 44–57). Columbia University Press.
Busby, E. (2019, 15 March). Climate strike: Give detentions to children who skip school to protest environmental catastrophe, headteachers' union leader says. *The Independent*. https://www.independent.co.uk/climate-change/news/climate-change-strike-protest-detention-school-teachers-a8824881.html
Butler, J. (2016). 'We, the people': Thoughts on freedom of assembly. In A. Badiou, B. Bosteels, P. Bourdieu, J. Butler, G. Didi-Huberman, J. Gladding, S. Khiari, K. Olson, & J. Rancière (Eds.), *What is a people?* (pp. 49–64). Columbia University Press.
Carr, W., & Hartnett, A. (1996). *Education and the struggle for democracy: The politics of educational ideas*. Open University Press.

Clayton, S. (2020). Climate anxiety: Psychological responses to climate change. *Journal of Anxiety Disorders, 74*, 102263. https://doi.org/10.1016/j.janxdis.2020.102263

Cox, S. (2020). *The new green deal and beyond: Ending the climate emergency while we still can.* City Lights Books.

Deese, R. S. (2019). *Climate change and the future of democracy.* Springer.

Dewey, J. (1899). *The school and society: Being three lectures.* University of Chicago Press.

Dorling, D. (2019). *Inequality and the 1%.* Verso.

Dyke, J., Watson, R., & Knorr, W. (2021, 22 April). Climate scientists: Concept of net zero is a dangerous trap. *The Conversation.* https://theconversation.com/climate-scientists-concept-of-net-zero-is-a-dangerous-trap-157368

Fischer, F. (2017). *Climate crisis and the democratic prospect: Participatory governance in sustainable communities.* Oxford University Press.

Flannery, T. (2020). *The climate cure: Solving the climate emergency in the era of COVID-19.* The Text Publishing Company.

Gaupp, F., Hall, J., Mitchell, D., & Dadson, S. (2019). Increasing risks of multiple breadbasket failure under 1.5 and 2°C global warming. *Agricultural Systems, 175,* 34–45. https://doi.org/10.1016/j.agsy.2019.05.010

Giroux, H. A. (2003). Public pedagogy and the politics of resistance: Notes on a critical theory of educational struggle. *Educational Philosophy and Theory, 35*(1), 5–16. https://doi.org/10.1111/1469-5812.00002

Giroux, H. A. (2004). Public pedagogy and the politics of neoliberalism: Making the political more pedagogical. *Policy Futures in Education, 2*(3–4), 494–503. https://doi.org/10.2304/pfie.2004.2.3.5

Giroux, H. A. (2005). Cultural studies in dark times: Public pedagogy and the challenge of neoliberalism. *Fast Capitalism, 1*(2), 75–86. https://doi.org/10.32855/fcapital.200502.010

Giroux, H. A. (2010). Neoliberalism as public pedagogy. In J. A. Sandlin, B. D. Schultz, & J. Burdick (Eds.), *Handbook of public pedagogy: Education and learning beyond schooling* (pp. 486–499). Routledge.

Giroux, H. A. (2016). *Schooling and the struggle for public life: Democracy's promise and education's challenge* (2nd ed.). Routledge.

Griffiths, E. (2014, 18 July). Carbon tax scrapped: PM Tony Abbott sees key election promise fulfilled after Senate votes for repeal. *ABC News.* https://www.abc.net.au/news/2014-07-17/carbon-tax-repealed-by-senate/5604246

Kaukko, M., Kemmis, S., Heikkinen, H. L. T., Kiilakoski, T., & Haswell, N. (2021). Learning to survive amidst nested crises: Can the coronavirus pandemic help US change educational practices to prepare for the impending eco-crisis? *Environmental Education Research.* https://doi.org/10.1080/13504622.2021.1962809

Klein, N. (2014). *This changes everything: Capitalism vs. the climate.* Alfred A. Knopf.

Lange, S., Volkholz, J., Geiger, T., Zhao, F., Vega, I., Veldkamp, T., Reyer, C. P. O., Warszawski, L., Huber, V., Jägermeyr, J., Schewe, J., Bresch, D. N., Büchner, M., Chang, J., Ciais, J., Dury, M., Emanuel, K., Folberth, C., Gerten, D., ... Frieler, F. (2020). Projecting exposure to extreme climate impact events across six event categories and three spatial scales. *Earth's Future, 8,* e2020EF001616. https://doi.org/10.1029/2020EF001616

Lannin, S. (2021, 27 May). Climate change activist wins against Exxon Mobil and Chevron, Shell loses Dutch court case. *ABC News.* https://www.abc.net.au/news/2021-05-27/climate-environment-shell-chevron-exxon/100169518

Lee, P. (2015). *Truth wars: The politics of climate change, military intervention and financial crisis.* Palgrave Macmillan.

Lenton, T. M., Rockström, J., Gaffney, O., Rahmstord, S., Richardson, K., Steffen, W., & Schellnhuber, H. J. (2019). Climate tipping points: Too risky to bet against. *Nature, 575*, 592–595. https://doi.org/10.1038/d41586-019-03595-0

Lewis, S. L., & Maslin, M. A. (2015). Defining the Anthropocene. *Nature, 519*, 171–180. https://doi.org/10.1038/nature14258

Mattheis, N. (2020). Unruly kids? Conceptualizing and defending youth disobedience. *European Journal of Political Theory*. https://doi.org/10.1177/1474885120918371

Mayes, E., & Hartup, M. (2021). News coverage of the School Strike for Climate movement in Australia: The politics of representing young Strikers' emotions. *Journal of Youth Studies*. https://doi.org/10.1080/13676261.2021.1929887

Mayes, E., & Hartup, M. (2022). Passion as politics: An analysis of Australian newspaper reporting of institutional responses to the school strikes for climate. In S. Riddle, A. Heffernan, & D. Bright (Eds.), *New perspectives on education for democracy: Creative responses to local and global challenges* (pp. 180–199). Routledge.

McGinn, M. (2019, 27 December). 2019's biggest pop-culture trend was climate anxiety. *Grist*. https://grist.org/politics/2019s-biggest-pop-culture-trend-was-climate-anxiety/

McLaren, P., & Farahmandpur, R. (2005). *Teaching against global capitalism and the new imperialism: A critical pedagogy*. Rowman & Littlefield Publishers.

Monbiot, G. (2016). *How did we get into this mess? Politics, equality, nature*. Verso.

Monbiot, G. (2018). *Out of the wreckage: A new politics for an age of crisis*. Verso.

Morton, A. (2021, 27 May). Australian court finds government has duty to protect young people from climate crisis. *The Guardian*. https://www.theguardian.com/australia-news/2021/may/27/australian-court-finds-government-has-duty-to-protect-young-people-from-climate-crisis

Mouffe, C. (1999). Deliberative democracy or agonistic pluralism? *Social Research, 66*(3), 745–758.

Mouffe, C. (2019). *For a left populism*. Verso.

Neela-Stock, S. (2019, 28 September). 5 young climate activists to follow beyond Greta Thunberg. *Mashable*. https://mashable.com/article/youth-climate-activists-greta-thunberg

Nothling, L. (2021). Queensland government responds to failure at coal-fired Callide power station by turning to battery power. *ABC News*. https://www.abc.net.au/news/2021-05-27/qld-renewable-energy-coal-fired-callide-power-station/100166152

O'Brien, A., & Baker, N. (2019, 20 September). Hundreds of thousands of Australians strike to protest climate inaction. *SBS News*. https://www.sbs.com.au/news/hundreds-of-thousands-of-australians-strike-to-protest-climate-inaction/c542f475-ac00-49fc-85ff-c698ea6c60b9

O'Neill, B. C., Oppenheimer, M., Warren, R., Hallegatte, S., Kopp, R. E., Pörtner, H. O., Scholes, R., Birkmann, J., Foden, W., Licker, R., Mach, K. J., Marbaix, P., Mastrandrea, M. D., Price, J., Takahashi, K., van Ypersele, J.-P., & Yobe, G. (2017). IPCC reasons for concern regarding climate change risks. *Nature Climate Change, 7*, 28–37. https://doi.org/10.1038/nclimate3179

Plato. (2007). *The republic*. Penguin Classics.

Ripple, W. J., Wolf, C., Newsome, T. M., Barnard, P., & Moomaw, W. R. (2020). World scientists' warning of a climate emergency. *BioScience, 70*(1), 8–12. https://doi.org/10.1093/biosci/biz088

Rowe, E., & Gerrard, J. (2019). Global social movements and dialogical pedagogy: Politics, power and process. In S. Riddle & M. W. Apple (Eds.), *Re-imagining education for democracy* (pp. 28–41). Routledge.

Schostak, J. (2019). 'Towards a society of equals': Democracy, education, cooperation and the practice of radical inclusion. *International Journal of Inclusive Education, 23*(11), 1103–1115. https://doi.org/10.1080/13603116.2019.1629161

Schostak, J., & Goodson, I. (2020). *Democracy, education and research: The struggle for public life*. Routledge.

Schwab, K., & Malleret, T. (2020). *COVID-19: The great reset*. Forum Publishing.

Seitzinger, S. P., Svedin, U., Crumley, C. L., Steffen, W., Abdulla, S. A., Alfsen, C., Broadgate, W. J., Biermann, F., Bondre, N. R., Dearing, J. A., Deutsch, L., Dhakal, S., Elmqvist, T., Farahbakhshazad, N., Gaffney, O., Haberl, H., Lavorel, S., Mbow, C., McMichael, A. J., ... Sugar, L. (2012). Planetary stewardship in an urbanizing world: Beyond city limits. *Ambio: A Journal of Environment and Society, 41*, 787–794. https://doi.org/10.1007/s13280-012-0353-7

Steffen, W., Rockström, J., Richardson, K., Lenton, T. M., Folke, C., Liverman, D., Summerhayes, C. P., Barnosky, A. D., Cornell, S. E., Crucifix, M., Donges, J. F., Fetzer, I., Lade, S. J., Scheffer, M., Winkelmann, R., & Schellnhuber, H. J. (2018). Trajectories of the Earth System in the Anthropocene. *Proceedings of the National Academy of Sciences of the United States of America, 115*(33), 8252–8259. https://doi.org/10.1073/pnas.1810141115

Swarbrick, C. (2021, 21 April). Youth protest is politics in its purest form. *New Zealand Herald*. https://www.nzherald.co.nz/nz/politics/chloe-swarbrick-youth-protest-is-politics-in-its-purest-form

Szolucha, A. (2016). *Real democracy in the Occupy movement: No stable ground*. Routledge.

Taylor, A. (2019). *Democracy may not exist, but we'll miss it when it's gone*. Verso.

Taylor, M., Watts, J., & Bartlett, J. (2019, 28 September). Climate crisis: 6 million people join latest wave of global protests. *The Guardian*. https://www.theguardian.com/environment/2019/sep/27/climate-crisis-6-million-people-join-latest-wave-of-worldwide-protests

Thunberg, G., Taylor, A., Neubauer, L., Gantois, K., De Wever, A., Charlier, A., Gillibrand, H., & Villasenor, A. (2019, 15 March). Think we should be at school? Today's climate strike is the biggest lesson of all. *The Guardian*. https://www.theguardian.com/commentisfree/2019/mar/15/school-climate-strike-greta-thunberg

Vicedo-Cabrera, A. M., Scovronick, N., Sera, F., Royé, D., Schneider, R., Tobias, A., Astrom, C., Guo, Y., Honda, Y., Hondula, D. M., Abrutzky, R., Tong, S., de Sousa Zanotti Stagliorio Coelho, M., Nascimento Saldiva, P. H., Lavigne, E., Matus Correa, P., Valdes Ortega, N., Kan, H., Osorio, S., ... Gasparrini, A. (2021). The burden of heat-related mortality attributable to recent human-induced climate change. *Nature Climate Change*. https://doi.org/10.1038/s41558-021-01058-x

Walker, C. (2020). Uneven solidarity: The school strikes for climate in global and intergenerational perspective. *Sustainable Earth, 3*, 5. https://doi.org/10.1186/s42055-020-00024-3

Ward, R. (2020, 3 March). Amelia Telford is sowing the seeds of climate action. *Victorian Women's Trust*. https://www.vwt.org.au/amelia-telford-is-sowing-the-seeds-of-climate-action/

Westbrook, T., & Fraser, A. (2019, 15 March). 'Worse than Voldermort': Global students' strike targets climate change. *Reuters*. https://www.reuters.com/article/us-climate-change-youth-idUSKCN1QW01S

Wu, J., Snell, G., & Samji, H. (2020). Climate anxiety in young people: A call to action. *The Lancet: Planetary Health, 4*(10), E435–E436. https://doi.org/10.1016/S2542-5196(20)30223-0

Young, E. (2020, 9 September). Eight young Australian teenagers have launched legal action to stop the expansion of a NSW coal mine. *SBS News*. https://www.sbs.com.au/news/eight-australian-teenagers-have-launched-legal-action-to-stop-the-expansion-of-a-nsw-coal-mine

Zakaria, F. (2020). *Ten lessons for a post-pandemic world*. W. W. Norton & Company.

5
PROPOSITIONS FOR DEMOCRATIC SCHOOLING

Introduction

In an essay published by the *New York Times* on the day of his funeral, US congressman and civil rights icon, John Lewis, argued that 'democracy is not a state. It is an act, and each generation must do its part to help build … a nation and world society at peace with itself' (Lewis, 2020). Democracy is an active and productive encounter with those around us; a commitment to collectively seek a meaningful engagement with the world. Democracy is not something that is done inside houses of parliament and the cloistered halls of power. It is an act of affirmation of life and of the shared bonds we have with one another. As such, democracy needs to be defended and defended again, articulated and re-articulated, imagined and re-imagined a thousand times over.

The continued atomisation of society into corporatised, marketised and commodified massified individualism (Rancière, 2006), the rise of China in the East and right-wing populism in the West, and the ubiquity of globalised market economics and digital surveillance capitalism (Gardels & Berggruen, 2019) have brought the contemporary institutions and practices of liberal democracy into a state of crisis, with substantial implications for the kind of societies in which we are able to live and work. Schwab and Malleret (2020) contended that:

> The fault lines of the world—most notably social divides, lack of fairness, absence of cooperation, failure of global governance and leadership—now lie exposed as never before, and people feel the time for reinvention has come. A new world will emerge, the contours of which are for us to both imagine and to draw.
>
> *(p. 11)*

DOI: 10.4324/9781003120063-5

A commitment to democracy requires that we include the future in our thinking (Taylor, 2019), and the clearest path to a future-oriented democracy is one that places children and young people at the centre of struggles for a more inclusive, responsible and sustainable society. Barber (1997) claimed that 'there is nothing sadder than a country that turns its back on its children, for in doing so it turns away from its own future' (p. 22). Yet, the steady erosion of social bonds, increasing mistrust, hate and fear, alongside a predatory capitalism that seeks to exploit young people for profit, while the climate crisis deepens, demonstrate that societies have done little to ensure that young people will inherit a world that is liveable, and a society in which they do not simply survive, but are able to thrive.

This book has considered some possible responses to the question of how schooling can be for democracy given the rise of anti-democratic forces during a time of global crisis. We face a time of unprecedented political, economic and social challenges. This book has examined the role of schooling as a critical and creative public project to reshape liberal–democratic societies in more socially just, sustainable, collective and active ways. Young people face a future of great uncertainty amid multiple, intersecting global crises, including increasing social and economic inequality, predatory globalised capitalism and neoliberal policymaking, the rise of post-truth discourses and the decay of trust, the global COVID-19 pandemic and a climate catastrophe, driving ecological collapse, mass extinction, food and water shortages and displacement. These crises present an enormous challenge, to which liberal–democratic governments and institutions have been unable to adequately respond. As an important social institution, schooling is supposed to provide young people with the skills and knowledge to participate fully in society, so this chapter considers how schooling can be for democracy in a time of global crisis. Drawing together the themes examined in this book, this chapter presents a series of propositions for democratic schooling in the twenty-first century.

Schooling for Democracy

It is going to be up to the young people of today to imagine and redraw the contours of this new world, as we emerge from the horrors of the COVID-19 pandemic and the deepening realisation of the existential threat of climate change takes hold. Business as usual will not suffice, no matter how many times political leaders and the corporate greenwashing machinery attempt to mollify and pacify the growing unrest. Young people can see right through the lies and obfuscation, and recognise that the gap in leadership will need to be filled by them. As such, it is more important than ever that a deeply democratic ethos is inculcated in education, especially schooling, and that thicker versions of democracy are made possible for all people, including those who are presently marginalised, disenfranchised and dispossessed of political, cultural and economic power. By opening schools to thicker democratic practices, it is possible to demonstrate a commitment to the formation of a more equal polity that is collectively and sustainably maintained (Riddle & Apple, 2019).

Important questions need to be asked regarding what kind of society we want schooling to foster and promote (Carr & Hartnett, 1996), including what the community desires of the education of its young, which means moving towards the language of possibility and to the 'terrain of hope and agency, to the sphere of struggle and action, one steeped in a vision which chooses life and offers constructive alternatives' (Aronowitz & Giroux, 1987, p. 19). While schooling is certainly not the only site of education, it is nevertheless an important public institution for providing education to young people (Angus, 1986; McMannon, 1997), which can either close down or open up the possibilities for more democratic modes of engagement. In the struggles for a more democratic society, it needs to be understood that the 'purpose of education is not given but is a constant topic for discussion and deliberation' (Biesta, 2010, p. 44).

The line of argument that has threaded throughout this book is that schooling should be *for* democracy because it sits at the heart of a more caring and inclusive society. However, successive governments of all kinds in Western liberal democracies have spent decades implementing neoliberal education reforms that have emphasised standardised testing, metrics of accountability and the policy rhetoric of responsibilisation, which places the blame for failure with individuals rather than acknowledging the systemic inequalities that fuel vastly unequal schooling access, opportunities and outcomes (Connell, 2013). As such, schooling has been mostly hollowed out to a technocratic method of preparing children and young adults to become workers within a globalised marketplace and a compliant consumer class.

Likewise, democracy has been hollowed out to the point where 'thin' forms of democratic participation are no better than a 'choice', which might be between almost identical political candidates in a triennial election cycle or between flavours of ice-cream in a super-sized megamart. These forms of consumerist choice give an illusion of freedom and participation, yet they are hollow and flimsy when held up to scrutiny. The democracy that has been boxed and sold to citizens in many parts of the world is not worthy of the name, seeking instead to restrain the democratic impulse and ensure that the massified individualism of contemporary consumer society keeps people docile and distracted. Despite the desire on the part of corporate oligarchs and the political class who sustain and enable them, business as usual cannot be allowed to continue. Something radical must be done to reclaim democracy and to refashion contemporary societies to be more equal, inclusive and caring.

Societies are faced with multiple complex challenges at the start of the third decade of the twenty-first century, which demand a range of creative responses, including how formal schooling is framed as a public project to produce critical and engaged young people with the collective commitment to tackle the effects of the global climate crisis, growing social and economic inequality, political instability, insecurity, fear and hate. Over the past two decades, liberal democracies in places such as Australia, the UK and US have witnessed the erosion of democratic institutions and principles, while also facing and failing to adequately respond to significant local and global challenges, including ecological breakdown, rising economic inequality, social unrest and political instability. There is substantial evidence of the corrosion of democracy and liberalism in many societies as sociopolitical and socioeconomic foundations are destabilised through multiple crises and conflicts in the first part of the twenty-first century. The current context is dangerous and uncertain, which makes it more important than ever to encourage widespread democratic participation and action.

This book has taken the challenge of education as its starting point—particularly schooling—being for democracy in a time of collapsing societal and environmental systems. It has considered the possible response of education to the multiple crises facing societies and the planet through the radical democratisation of schooling. Schools have long been studied as potential sites of democracy, although with mixed success. The current context of global crisis demands a more radical set of democratic principles and practices, which can be nurtured within schools and other formal and informal sites of education. It also addresses the tensions and potential contradictions in schools, which can easily operate as social sites of exclusion and 'citizenship building', which standardise and reduce the capacity for young people to express themselves in democratic ways (Apple, 2004). There are multiple examples of young people demonstrating their great capacity for democratic engagement, whether through direct action, civil disobedience and resistance, which demonstrate hope and the potential of collective action. However, the role of schooling is intimately bound up with the experiences, knowledge and capacity for creativity and criticality of young people. The daily practices of learners, educators, leaders, communities and societies can work towards collective well-being, increased civic participation and a common commitment to an ecologically sustainable engagement with the planet. It is important to centre the struggles and engagements of young people—especially those who are marginalised and minoritised—which demonstrate productive new expressions of hopeful encounters in local and global communities, and produce a plurality of possibilities regarding more democratic ways of living and learning together (Apple, 2013).

Of course, schools are not automatically democratic places, and are often intentionally designed to be undemocratic social institutions in which 'young people learn to regulate and control their behaviours, to follow rules and engage in a multitude of compliances to authority' (Riddle & Cleaver, 2017, p. 117). Indeed, there is some argument that under capitalism, schools cannot become spaces of social empowerment and democratic enfranchisement (Aronowitz & Giroux, 1987). Schools have long played an active role in reinforcing social and cultural relations (Connell, 1993) and being part of the machinery of reproducing inequalities as normative socialising institutions. Schools can 'perform economic and cultural functions and embody ideological rules that both preserve and enhance an existing set of structural relations. These relations operate at a fundamental level to help some groups and serve as a barrier to others' (Apple, 2004, p. 62). However, it does not have to be this way. As Gutmann (1999) argued, just because schools are not ideal democratic spaces and democratic societies are not perfectly democratic, 'should not disenchant us either with schooling or democracy' (p. 94). Rather, we should firmly demand that schools be reclaimed as democratic spaces for building community life, not simply places where children are skilled and drilled for future roles in the process of economic production and consumption. We need to reclaim schooling as a site of radical democratic education for a more caring, sustainable and inclusive future:

> A radical education built on the value of democracy and a multidimensional understanding of democracy expresses itself in a variety of ways: in the way educational politics and policy-making are conducted; in the governance of schools and decision-making large and small; in processes of learning and concepts of knowledge adopted; in ways of evaluation; and in everyday practices and relationships.
>
> *(Fielding & Moss, 2010, p. 42)*

Perhaps Counts (1932) was onto something nearly a century ago, when arguing that schools need to actively inscribe democratic values and civic virtue into the education experiences of young people as a means to oppose the closing down and reactivity of social conservatism and oppression. More recently, Carr and Thésée (2019) argued that 'the time for transformative education to accompany a more meaningful democracy has arrived' (p. 255). Therefore, three broad propositions for democratic schooling in the twenty-first century are outlined here, which might help to better provide young people with the skills, knowledge and creative and critical capacities to meaningfully engage in active democratic activity:

1. Schooling should support the development of rich critical capacities, through which young people can understand the discourses of truth, power and ideology that work on them through the political, economic and cultural systems of neoliberalism, capitalism and democracy in contemporary societies.
2. Schooling should develop the 'democratic impulse' in young people through the lived practice of a relational pedagogy, in which students are brought 'into relation' with their learning in meaningful and connected ways.
3. Schooling should provide a site for community engagement and dialogue to provide young people and their communities with a public space of collective and collaborative struggle against de-democratisation in local and global contexts.

Nurturing Critical and Creative Activist–Learners

A schooling that is for democracy must hold as a first principle the commitment to the development of young people's rich critical capacities. To do so is to ensure a deep understanding and powerful mastery over the regimes of truth, cultural and social discourses, flows of power and ideological foundations of the political, economic and cultural systems of contemporary capitalist and neoliberal societies. By going beyond teaching students to read the word, so that they can read the world (Freire, 1972), a critical orientation to schooling places the meaning-making practices and critical–cultural operations of texts, language and their production of knowledge and truth at the heart of education (Beane & Apple, 2007). The inculcation of a critical orientation towards society and its institutions and practices is an important part of a schooling that is for democracy. Importantly, 'those committed to creating democratic schools also understand that doing so involves more than the education of the young. Democratic schools are meant to be democratic places' (Beane & Apple, 2007, p. 8). Further, public schools must be committed to plurality and diversity as part of their mission to establish a commitment to the public good (Barber, 1997). It is not enough to educate young people; they must be supported and guided in the process of becoming critical, creative and capable citizens and powerful agents of social change who form a public:

> In attaching not just education but *public* education, critics are attacking the very foundation of our democratic civic culture. Public schools are not merely schools *for* the public, but schools of publicness: institutions where we learn what it means to *be* a public and start down the road toward common national and civic identity. They are the forges of our citizenship and the bedrock of our democracy.
>
> *(Barber, 1997, p. 22)*

Counts (1932) understood that the rapidity of change would continue to accelerate—observations that pre-dated modern high-speed global telecommunications and information technologies, robotics, AI and automation by almost a century—which would require an adaptive and agile schooling that engages with, and seeks to reshape the world (for the better). Dewey (1902) argued that critical self-realisation of the learner within the context of the democratic community was the highest goal of schooling, which has perhaps become only more important. The construction of knowledge and social reproduction through school curriculum has been a perennial battleground of ideological confrontation between progressives and conservatives, through which curriculum has shaped and been shaped by wider social forces (Apple, 2004).

Further, Aronowitz and Giroux (1987) argued that schools should be institutions that foster democracy by promoting the development of a 'critical culture and social practices that allow students and others to view society with an analytical eye' (p. 205), in which critical literacy and civic courage are part of the pedagogical and curricular bedrock of schooling. However, current formations of schooling have largely sidelined democratic modes of social encounters to fairly staid renditions of civics and citizenship curriculum, in which students learn about the structures and institutions of parliaments, representative democracy, elections and the importance of checks and balances between the executive, legislature and judiciary. Instead, what Aronowitz and Giroux, alongside other critical progressive educators have argued for is a radical reconfiguration of schooling so that the democratic spirit is nurtured in young people through critical and creative acts of activist civic engagement. This kind of learning takes place in the world, not in the revision questions at the end of a civics text book chapter. Fielding and Moss (2010) were unforgiving in their assessment of current schooling modalities and critical engagement with the world, claiming that:

> Current education and schooling have hardly begun to engage with the changes that are needed to exploit the opportunities or address the dangers confronting us. Indeed by their continuing entanglement in the current but bankrupt system preaching rising consumption, increasing growth, spreading commodification and intensified competition, they are part of the problem rather than the solution.
>
> (p. 64)

If we want to reshape schooling to be for democracy rather than a site of enculturation into the present hegemonic forms of social, economic and political organisation, it is important to nurture the critical and creative capacities of young people, but not simply in a theoretical, abstracted fashion. There needs to be opportunities for real, thick, activist forms of democratic participation and civic action built into school curriculum, which supports students to become critical agents who actively negotiate the power relationships within schools, communities and broader society. Teachers must engage students in a critical politics of difference as part of the commitment to developing a tradition of radical democracy (Aronowitz & Giroux, 1991). As Giroux (2009) has argued, this approach requires a pedagogical impulse that refuses to blindly serve the status quo of hegemonic forms of curriculum, but to open up spaces within classroom discourse for dissent, agonistic encounters and radical rethinking of the relationships between learners and their learning. To do so is to engage in the kind of praxis of inquiry and action that Freire (1972) argued for, in which knowledge emerges through 'invention and re-invention, through the restless, impatient, continuing, hopeful inquiry human beings pursue in the world, with the world, and with each other' (p. 46). Democracy is lived, not simply learned.

Arblaster (1972) claimed that education should not be indoctrination, but rather forms an essential critical function to encourage young people to question, to be inquisitive, to be sceptical, to doubt and to imagine how things might be otherwise. In this formulation, education is a subversive force, which stands in opposition to the taken-for-grantedness of hegemonic power structures, political and economic institutions, and the formation of social and cultural practices. Importantly, democracy as a way of living together in more inclusive and collaborative ways requires the constant struggle against hegemonic power in a commitment to maintaining the struggle of oppositional politics as a lived form of democratic expression (Aronowitz & Giroux, 1991). Democracy does not happen by chance, but through the lasting commitments of people within communities who seek to work together towards a notion of the collective good, the generation of a public that is inclusive of everyone, and which seeks to sustain society in ways that support health, economic equality, social belonging and cultural vitality.

Young people have demonstrated the power of activist struggles, political resistance and civil disobedience through movements such as the School Strikes for Climate (see Chapter 4), which bring young people to the centre of the debate about the kinds of economic and political structures that we need in a rapidly warming world and a disintegrating politics of mistrust and rising authoritarianism. The public pedagogy afforded by such struggles speaks to the importance of acts of resistance and reframing through education, which can reclaim public institutions for democracy (Giroux, 2003, 2004, 2005, 2010). Schools can play an important role in the development of critical literacy to support the activist learning of young people:

> Critical literacy in this case points to forms of knowledge and social practice that take seriously the notion of school democracy. Moreover, it points to the need to develop a real defense of schools as institutions which perform a public service, a service defined by the imperative to create a literate, democratic and active citizenry—in this case, citizens who would be self-governing and actively involved in the shaping of public welfare.
> *(Aronowitz & Giroux, 1987, p. 134)*

Supporting students to develop a repertoire of critical capacities is a key part of schooling for democracy because it enables young people to understand the workings of power through language, political, social and cultural institutions and practices. Amsler (2015) argued that being able to engage critically with the world allows the orientation of 'thinking away from abstract forces that we presume exist beyond ourselves and focus on the practice of possibility itself' (p. 58). It is within the realms of the possible that schooling for democracy operates, by seeking to fashion young people as active agents of social and political change, rather than positioning them as future workers and consumers within market-oriented economies. Such an orientation to a critical pedagogy of activist inquiry requires collective and dialogical engagement with teachers and students in a critical relationship with understanding how power marginalises, oppresses and exploits through language, discourse, politics, economics and culture, which is 'animated by a passionate and critical-minded optimism' (McLaren &

Farahmandpur, 2005, p. 9). As such, one of the principled tasks of critically minded teachers is to orient schooling curriculum towards more socially just futures, in which equality and freedom sit alongside a broader democratic project and through which students are already working together as powerfully engaged critical citizens. In support of critical modes of pedagogical relationships with young people, Giroux (2010) argued that:

> Critical pedagogy attempts to understand how power works through the production, distribution, and consumption of knowledge within particular institutional contexts and seeks to constitute students as informed subjects and social agents. In this instance, the issues of how identities, values, and desires are shaped in the classroom are the grounds of politics. Critical pedagogy is thus invested in both the practice of self-criticism about the values that inform teaching and a critical self-consciousness regarding what it means to equip students with analytical skills to be self-reflective about the knowledge and values they confront in classrooms. Moreover, such a pedagogy attempts not only to provide the conditions for students to understand texts and different modes of intelligibility, but also opens up new avenues for them to make better moral judgments that will enable them to assume some sense of responsibility to the other in light of those judgments.
>
> (p. 717)

The creation of a democratic culture in the classroom requires the collective passions of students and teachers for the common good, equality, recognition, individuality, openness and a sense of civic purpose and duty (Ferrara, 2014). These passions are built from the critical and creative capacities of young people to think and to live differently with each other, which does not fall into the trap of reproducing the social, economic and political inequalities that exist within the present system. As radical agents for change, young people require the critical literacy to read the word and the world, and then to purposefully intervene in ways that are collaborative and sustainable, inclusive and caring. Through these acts, schooling for democracy can offer young people the opportunity to engage in radical collective social transformation, which can respond to the complex challenges facing them.

Putting Relational Pedagogy at the Heart of Classrooms

Schools should seek ways to develop, nurture and sustain young people's democratic impulse through rich encounters within the lived practices and discourses of schooling, with a particular emphasis on bringing them into relation with their learning in critical and creative ways through meaningful engagement with the curriculum. Recentring curriculum and pedagogy to radically extend democratic principles and to engage in forms of community building and struggles for reclaiming public spaces and institutions requires a pedagogical relationality that builds upon difference and multiple ways of being together (Aronowitz & Giroux, 1991). As part of the argument for a more relational approach to schooling, Giroux (2016) argued for the importance of socially critical teaching and learning:

> In opposition to the rising tide of authoritarianism, educators must make a case for linking learning to social change, pluralizing and critically engaging the diverse sites where public pedagogy takes place, and must make clear that every sphere of social life is open to political contestation and constitutes a crucial site of political, social, and cultural struggle in the attempt to forge the knowledge, identifications, affective investments, and social relations that constitute a political subject and social agent capable of energizing and spreading the basis of a global radical democracy.
>
> *(p. xxvii)*

Connell (1993) argued nearly 30 years ago that social justice should sit at the heart of schooling, by reconfiguring mainstream curriculum and pedagogy to 'embody the interests of the least advantaged' (p. 44). The project of reshaping the curriculum to be counter-hegemonic is a key feature of relational modes of pedagogy, including culturally relevant and sustaining pedagogies. Such a form of curricular justice is central to ensuring more equitable access for all young people to schooling that meaningfully connects with their lives and experiences, while also fostering democratic participation, civic participation and social inclusion (Mills et al., 2021). To open up possibilities for encountering difference and socially just teaching and learning, the goal of curricular justice is to fashion a curriculum that is built from the experiences, cultures, histories and representations of people and places that connect meaningfully to the lives of those who are least advantaged by society's current formations. For example, 'socially just curriculum will draw extensively on Indigenous knowledge, working class experience, women's experience, immigrant cultures, multiple languages, and so on; aiming for richness rather than testability' (Connell, 2012, p. 682).

When students, teachers and curriculum are brought into close pedagogical relation with each other, there is a democratic nature to the encounters that play out in the classroom and more broadly in education contexts (Hickey et al., 2022). There is a growing body of literature that has demonstrated the critical, creative and democratic possibilities opened up through relational pedagogies (e.g., Bingham & Sidorkin, 2004; Edwards-Groves et al., 2010; Hickey & Riddle, 2021; Hickey et al., 2021; Ljungblad, 2019; Sidorkin, 2000). Relational pedagogies arise from a participatory ethic of 'being in relation', which can activate inclusive, socially just learning for young people (Hickey & Riddle, 2021).

Relational modalities in the classroom have much to learn from the contemporary literature on culturally relevant and cultural sustaining pedagogies (e.g., Bishop & Vass, 2020; Ladson-Billings, 1995, 2014, 2021; McCarty & Lee,

2014; Morrison et al., 2019; Paris, 2012, 2021), which seek to recentre school curriculum to engage with the experiences and knowledges of marginalised and minoritised communities, including First Nations, Black, Latinx, Pacific Islander and other culturally and linguistically diverse learners. Culturally responsive and sustaining pedagogies aim to reimagine and transform schooling for racial, decolonial and climate justice (Paris, 2021), through which education and educators move from the centre to the margins through a pedagogical de-centring to foreground students' cultural practice (Ladson-Billings, 2021). Importantly, culturally sustaining pedagogies seek 'to perpetuate and foster—to sustain—linguistic, literate, and cultural pluralism as part of the democratic project of schooling' (Paris, 2012, p. 95). Further, culturally responsive pedagogies work towards productive cultural, social and linguistic pluralism as a 'fundamental feature of the democratic ethos (whether as an ethic of community living or a structure of government), and as a necessary component of quality education' (Gay, 2015, p. 125).

There is little doubt that 'any move towards a democratic education should countenance the ways in which students and teachers come to the pedagogical encounter' (Hickey et al., 2022, p. 209), which places relational modalities of teaching and learning at the centre of a schooling that is for democracy. Not a democracy that is to be experienced outside of the classroom setting, but one in which young people are able to engage in acts of democratic equality as a daily part of their schooling. This speaks to Dewey's (1899) argument that schooling is not a preparation for life, but a space for young people to live their lives. Therefore, putting relational pedagogy at the heart of the classroom can better serve to support young people in becoming critical and creative citizens, who are able to work together on collective problems and generate collaborative solutions. Relational pedagogy supports radical education through responsibility towards each other, which is driven by an ethics of care and an ethics of encounter (Fielding & Moss, 2010). Rancière (1991) claimed that a politics of educational emancipation requires a radical equality and relationality between the learner, the book (i.e., the curriculum) and the teacher, from which critical learning can emerge. Equality must be the starting point of such a relational pedagogy if there is to any chance of a democratic encounter (Rancière, 2006) built into the act of learning and teaching. Contemporary forms of neoliberalised schooling begin from the fundamental inequality between the one who educates and the one who is educated (Biesta, 2013), which does not allow for a democratic encounter between educator and learner as equals.

Additionally, Zembylas (2020) argued that democracy is an affective activity, which is a form of social practices lived inside and outside the classroom, rather than a set of skills and knowledge taught through formal curriculum to be applied elsewhere. For example, a study in Turkey found that relational pedagogies in which students were affectively engaged promoted democratic learning, which had important implications for broader democratisation efforts (Altinyelken, 2015). Given the clear and present threat to Turkish democracy by rising authoritarianism and increasing political division, the importance of pedagogies that encourage reflexive, critical and responsive engagement by young people in society seems more imperative than ever. Democratic education is more than learning about democracy for a future democratic engagement, but rather a set of social practices built into the fabric of curriculum and pedagogy, in which democratic values are cultivated in critical and constructive ways (Zembylas, 2020) to further the democratic project. In arguing for education as the practice of freedom, Freire (1972) claimed that it is in relation with the world that education can best serve its emancipatory purpose, and that through dialogue that the world becomes named and understood so that it might become transformed, and that a horizontal relationship of trust, love and humility are able to be formed. Freire (1972) continued:

> Only dialogue, which requires critical thinking, is also capable of generating critical thinking. Without dialogue there is no communication, and without communication there can be no true education. Education which is able to resolve the contradiction between teacher and student takes place in a situation in which both address their act of cognition to the object by which they are mediated.
>
> *(p. 65)*

The role of the teacher is to open up the pedagogical encounter to radical equality, care and relationality, so that students can practice their democratic activism in a safe and supportive environment. Teachers must do more than teach the curriculum; they need to be transformative intellectuals who seek to broaden the democratic nature of education by mobilising schooling as a public institution with the aim of generating a more socially just society. Giroux (2016) argued that 'by linking schooling to wider social movements, teachers can begin to redefine the nature and importance of pedagogical struggle and thereby provide the basis to fight for forms of emancipatory authority as a foundation for the establishment of freedom and justice' (pp. 110–111).

Schools as Public Sites of Community Democratisation

> Each generation is inclined to educate its young so as to get along in the present world instead of with a view to the proper end of education: the promotion of the best possible realization of humanity.
>
> *(Dewey, 1916, p. 111)*

Schools are important and genuine sites of community life, and not simply places in which young people go to learn curriculum. Indeed, 'social justice and democratic community form a core of the moral purpose of schools' (Riddle & Cleaver, 2017, p. 36). As such, schools have an important role to play in the democratisation and re-democratisation of society, as well as in actively resisting de-democratisation through acts of collective democratic participation. Schools provide a public site of community engagement and dialogue, which can connect to and work with the collective struggles for equality and liberty, anti-racism and decolonialisation of political, economic, social and cultural life. As Dewey (1899) argued over a century ago, societies are held together by common bonds through the shared commitment to common needs and aims through 'a growing interchange of thought and growing unity of sympathetic feeling' (p. 27), which requires radically rethinking the structures and institutions of common life to be more inclusive, caring and just.

Drawing on Bernstein's notion of pedagogic rights—enhancement, inclusion and participation—Heimans et al. (2021) proposed that education could improve the possibilities of democracy by pushing 'democracy back into education itself, to open education up to "becoming public(s)", against the now widespread exogenous and endogenous privatisations' (p. 9). This is important work, which must occur inside and outside the school grounds, to develop more democratic modes of civic participation. There are hopeful examples, through the accounts of teachers, students, their families and communities, engaging in collective struggles for re-democratisation and reclaiming of public spaces and institutions (e.g., Apple, 2018; Apple & Beane, 2007; Heggart & Kolber, 2022; Riddle & Apple, 2019; Riddle et al., 2022a). There is clearly an urgency to the 'urgent need to both resist authoritarian educational reforms that seek to minimise the freedoms of teachers and students while also finding new expressions of hopeful education in both local and global communities' (Riddle, 2019, p. 6).

Situating the school as a site of 'becoming public(s)' and a place of radically inclusive education enables the bringing together of a multiplicity of voices and perspectives, articulating a logic of equality and freedom from which new alternatives and socially just futures can be framed as genuine alternatives to the hierarchical inequalities of globalised capitalism, alongside the constraining forces of neoconservatism and neoliberalism (Schostak, 2019). The commitment to the school as a radical democratic space for communities to engage in civil and civic encounters of equality (Goodlad, 1979, 2011) is an important step in the direction of community democratisation through schools as public institutions.

Further, Ball and Collette-Sabé (2021) argued that the school as a normative institution also requires significant rethinking, in that 'the issue is whether the school is a solution to the problem of education or rather a constant and ineluctable source of educational problems' (p. 2). Schools can certainly be both part of the problem and part of the solution. Given that there is likely to be limited political and social desire to remove schooling as a formal site of education, some kind of compromise is required. Perhaps Rancière's (2006, 2010) arguments about democracy offer some clues for a way forward for schooling as an important community site of democratisation, in that democracy is actually found, not in the machinations of government nor the voting habits of the electorate, but within the encounters between people in which equality of participation enables the act of democracy to emerge. As such, schools *can* be places of radical and transformative democratic activity in which teachers collaborate with communities beyond the classroom because if educators seek to 'have any significant effect on the unequal economic, political, and social arrangements that plague schools and the wider society, they have no choice but to actively engage in the struggle for democracy with groups *outside* their classrooms' (Giroux, 2016, p. 110).

There is powerful potential in schools working within communities of democratic practice, in which 'education has the capacity to undercut the institutional supports to inequality and elite power by creating a different field of relationships between free and equal individuals learning and working together to create their social projects in common' (Schostak & Goodson, 2020, p. 113). Schools can become public sites of community democratisation that encourage a vibrant and inclusive public space in which young people can work as important members of the community towards the common public good (Fielding, 2007). The importance of developing common bonds of civic commitment to public debate and public modes of living together cannot be overstated in the struggle to reclaim the political, economic and social systems that govern societies. The multiple crises facing the world require more collective and democratic modes of engagement if we are to find a path that leads to sustainable futures for life on the planet.

Towards a New Democratic Horizon

Schooling for democracy should be part of the project to engage in a multiplicity of democratic practices, through which young people are able to become critical and creative agents of democratic change within their local and global communities through youth-led democratic movements. The emancipatory possibility of a democratic ethos built on the premise of radical equality and productive dissensus (Biesta, 2010) is one that opens up new horizons for a future that is more democratic, inclusive and sustainable, both on the social and planetary level (Ferrara, 2014). Drawing on the work of Mouffe (1993, 1999, 2019) and Rancière (2006, 2010), radical democracy requires the acceptance that political life is built from productive conflict, through dissensus and agonism. In this formulation of democracy, dissensus is an unpredictable and disruptive process, challenging existing consensus to form new consensus and antagonisms (Taylor, 2019), which can lead to new ways of being together in response to a multiplicity of difference of peoples, perspectives and practices within democracy. Perhaps in doing so, we can seek out new forms of democracy (Biesta, 2014). Of course, while there is no single definition of radical democracy, at its core, radical democracy is a political commitment to 'liberate possibilities from the imposition of all "false necessity"; to maintain an anarchic scepticism towards both truth and power, and to facilitate the practical work that these commitments require' (Amsler, 2015, p. 73).

Importantly, Sant (2021) argued that 'it is neither possible nor desirable to regulate differences and group decision-making in such a way that everybody is truly satisfied. Consensual agreements are the deceiving ways to refer to situations where the rule of the stronger is applied and the weaker is silenced'

(p. 25). The point is not to steadfastly agree, but to ensure that a plurality of voices is heard and empowered through democratic engagement. The aim is not to achieve some blind Rousseau-styled collective will, but to open up the possibilities of the democratic encounter to difference. Further, Mouffe (1993) argued for a new hegemony of democratic values, which requires the multiplication of democratic practices, institutions and values in more diverse ways, so that a multiplicity of democratic values and subjective positions can be established through the embedding of radical equality in democratic practice, which can be defended and extended. Additionally, she claimed that 'a project of radical and plural democracy … requires the existence of multiplicity, of plurality and of conflict, and sees in them the *raison d'être* of politics' (Mouffe, 1993, p. 18).

The kind of radical and plural democracy espoused by Mouffe (1993, 2019) and Rancière (2006, 2010) is not a project of the future, but rather the here and now. Teachers and students within schools can practice acts of radical democracy through the assumption of equality in curriculum and pedagogy in the here and now. Inequality is not something to be tackled 'out there', but in the pedagogical encounter itself, through which education is an act not of knowledge transmission but a way of living with each other to build new knowledges and understandings through close social bonds and a commitment to equality in all aspects of life. Biesta (2013) described the importance of a democratic subjectification and pedagogisation through education, in which democracy is the 'claim' for equality. Such a claim to equality embodies two core democratic principles: That anyone can participate in democratic activity, and that those who do so are freely equal (Waldron, 2010).

It is not simply a question of seeking *more* democracy, in that schools can be places of democratic participation and action where they previously were not, but that we can rethink democracy itself to engage in different democratic modes of governance and encounters within communities and societies that support not only the principles of equality and liberty, but are wholly committed to ensuring sustainable ecological futures. Biesta (2014) suggested that one way to approach the thinking differently of democracy is to consider it an ongoing and never-ending experiment, which is always partially realised, but remains open to new horizons of possibility. Mouffe (1993) argued that a pluralist democracy contains an inherent paradox because conflict and antagonism are conditions of both possibility and impossibility of democracy being fully realised. As such, democracy is always in a state of becoming, rather than being a fixed point of social and political organisation. This is its strength. Radical democracy works at the limits of the democratic horizon:

> Thresholds, boundaries, edges, borders, borderlands, horizons, zones of proximal development, liminal spaces, and symbolic and material frontiers—all these concepts sensitize us to the fundamental problem of possibility. They are also important within radical democratic politics, which gravitates towards fronts of possibility by striving to disclose,

> unsettle, dissolve, transgress, transform, relocate and refuse contingent limitations; challenge static concepts, identities and relationships; refuse necessities imposed by domination; encourage encounters with difference that deepen respect for common life; and visualize possibilities that do not yet quite exist.
>
> *(Amsler, 2015, p. 58)*

The commitment to schooling for democracy is one that requires understanding of impossibility of creating fully democratic modes within institutions that have long prepared young people for socialisation into the economic, cultural and political systems of the present social formations. To become places in which radical democratic action can take place as part of the firmament of schooling requires a kind of unschooling process to take place, in which schools could potentially become no longer recognisably schools (Ball & Collette-Sabé, 2021). However, this should not prevent educators and students from seeking to make schools more democratic spaces regardless because the current context of global crisis demands action. We can, and must, imagine our societies differently, and then act upon those reimaginings. As Mouffe (2019) argued, 'despite the claim of many liberal theorists that political liberalism necessarily entails economic liberalism and that a democratic society requires a capitalist economy, it is clear that there is no necessary relationship between capitalism and liberal democracy' (p. 48).

The hegemony of globalised capitalism and its attendant neoliberal political formulations and neoconservative social forces can be undone and replaced with something else. For example, Mouffe (2019) called for a left populism as part of the project to establish a new hegemonic order within a liberal–democratic framework, which is pluralist and allows for a heterogeneity of economic and social formations in opposition to neoliberalism and capitalism. Certainly, 'the process of recovering and radicalizing democratic institutions will no doubt include moments of rupture and a confrontation with the dominant economic interests, but it does not require relinquishing the liberal–democratic principles of legitimacy' (Mouffe, 2019, p. 45). There is no need for a destructive revolutionary inversion of society, but a reimagining of the principles, policies and practices of social, economic and political institutions and how they function within liberal–democratic societies to ensure that they are more inclusive, caring and sustainable, with a commitment to a future in which everyone can thrive and participate fully in public life of the commons, which is in harmony with ecological systems and other life on the planet.

Despite the powerful effects of direct democratic action through social movements such as the Occupy movement, Extinction Rebellion and the School Strikes for Climate, there is a powerful inertia built into the current neoliberal and global capital settings of contemporary liberal–democratic societies, subsuming these explosive forms of collective will and eventually commodifying them through the sales of merchandise, social media memes and outrage performed on digital platforms alongside targeted advertising driven by algorithms based on the activities and preferences of the very same people protesting against the encroachment of surveillance capitalism, predation by corporate oligarchies and the increasing lust of multinational fossil fuel companies to extract as much as they can before the political will finally turns against them. Instead, Srnicek and Williams (2016) claimed that large mobilisations of collective democratic will need to move beyond folk politics and the mobilisation of people and passions to broader movements that can generate long-lasting forces that can supersede, rather than simply resist, globalised capitalism. Mouffe (2019) suggested that the time for new radical democratic forms has come because 'the current crisis of the neoliberal hegemonic formation offers the possibility of intervening to establish a different order' (p. 35). However, Mouffe (2019) warned that 'while the crisis of neoliberalism provides the opportunity to construct a new hegemonic order, there is no guarantee that this new order will bring about significant democratic advances and it might even be of an authoritarian nature' (p. 35). Such a warning should be heeded, although the signs of youth-led democratic change through collective movements such as the School Strikes for Climate provide hopeful glimpses of the possibilities of a new democratic horizon.

Schooling for democracy should be part of the project for constructing a new hegemonic order, which holds plurality, multiplicity and a firm commitment to equality and liberty alongside sustainable ecological futures and a democracy built from dissensus and agonism. There is hope in this project, which is an essential requirement for reimagining society towards a hopeful future (Bauman, 2004). As Arendt (1969) argued over half a century ago:

> Education is the point at which we decide whether we love the world enough to assume responsibility for it and by the same token save it from that ruin which, except for renewal, except for the corning of the new and young, would be inevitable. And education, too, is where we decide whether we love our children enough not to expel them from our world and leave them to their own devices, nor to strike from their hands their chance of undertaking something new, something unforeseen by us, but to prepare them in advance for the task of renewing a common world.
>
> (p. 196)

There is an urgent need to renew the common world, which requires action from below, the young, the marginalised and disenfranchised. They are the ones who will change the world, not the elites and their corporate monopolies (Monbiot, 2016). Young people understand that things cannot stay as they are, and they possess a planetary sense of responsibility, which acknowledges 'none of us can any longer seek and find private shelter from storms that originate in any part of the globe' (Bauman, 2004, p. 66). The radical democratisation of schools and other sites of public life can support young people in the re-democratisation of society. As Giroux (2016) articulated, a revitalised public philosophy is required, which grounds democracy in the forms of community solidarity, critical citizenship and public life that can expand the horizons of human possibilities for life, freedom and sustainable engagement with the world. Progressive and radical educators can support young people in their struggles against global capitalism and entrenched inequality, racism, greed, hate and fear, by working within their communities towards the pedagogisation of democracy through acts of solidarity and expressions of radical equality and democratic action (Aronowitz, 2008). The survival of democracy, and perhaps human society, depends upon a commitment to the struggles of communities to address local and global crises.

We need new ways of creatively and critically thinking about democracy, enacting democracy through relational pedagogies and activist curriculum inside and outside the school classroom, and engaging in acts of radical democratic collectivity if we are to have any hope of not simply surviving, but thriving during the twenty-first century. There is no doubt that 'we require new understandings of civic belonging and democratic modes of living together in a fragile world, in which our shared obligation to each other is the first principle underpinning education' (Riddle et al., 2022b, p. 8). Love, hope and solidarity must sit at the heart of a project to rethink democracy for a more ecologically sustainable and socially inclusive world.

Perhaps it remains that 'the present situation is also freighted with hope and promise. The age is pregnant with possibilities. There lies within our grasp the most humane, the most beautiful, the most majestic civilization ever fashioned by any people' (Counts, 1932, p. 35). However, we must ensure that we do not fashion our own Omelas, from which young people will have no choice but to either accept the terrible price of our economic prosperity—for those who benefit from the present systems of capitalist exploitation, that is—or to disconnect, to walk away and abrogate responsibility for the state of affairs. The complex set of contemporary crises facing us requires active and engaged communities, of which young people are a central part, to participate in acts of rebellion and disruption against the hegemonic forces of capitalism, neoliberalism and neoconservatism, which seek to further plunder and tear apart the ecological and social fabric of life on this place.

We cannot accept that there are no alternatives to our present societal moment, in which neoliberalism, neoconservatism and predatory global capitalism are taken for granted as the way things are. Things can, and must be different. We are living in a time of multiple, intersecting global crises, which has brought human societies, ecological systems and life on the planet to a critical juncture. We are facing a century of somewhere between 2°C and 4°C warming, which will cause—and is already causing—calamitous effects on the environmental and human systems we need to survive. We are faced with unacceptable levels of social and economic inequality, in which an elite class are able to take joyrides into space in their private spacecraft, while millions suffer from poverty, without adequate food and water, healthcare or access to primary education. Global capitalism, with its predatory impulse and exploitation, has combined with economic austerity and social atomisation of neoliberal policymaking over the past three decades, to ensure that the gulf between those who have and those who have not continues to widen (Street, 2015). The rise of a politics of hate, fear and mistrust has unravelled important bonds of community and social cohesion, alongside the deleterious effects of post-truth discourses and the rise of populism as a fundamental threat to freedom and equality. It is not just democracy at stake, but a future in which young people can thrive and collaborate together on important acts of social, cultural, political and economic progress.

Schools are no doubt imperfect institutions, yet they must be part of any reimagining of education that is going to nurture and develop young people's critical and creative capacity for radical democratic engagement and support their desire to change society to be more inclusive, caring and sustainable. We owe it to our children, and the children who are yet to come, to work together as educators, activists, parents and community members, to reclaim public spaces of engagement and community belonging, to reinscribe them with civil action and civic virtue, and to commit to the struggle to ensure that the crises of the twenty-first century can be met head-on by opening up the horizon to a multiplicity of democratic possibilities. This is the purpose and promise of schooling for democracy.

References

Altinyelken, H. K. (2015). Democratising Turkey through student-centred pedagogy: Opportunities and pitfalls. *Comparative Education*, *51*(4), 484–501. https://doi.org/10.1080/03050068.2015.1081794

Amsler, S. S. (2015). *The education of radical democracy*. Routledge.

Angus, L. (1986). *Schooling for social order: Democracy, equality and social mobility in education*. Deakin University Press.

Apple, M. W. (2004). *Ideology and curriculum* (2nd ed.). RoutledgeFalmer.

Apple, M. W. (2013). *Knowledge, power and education*. Routledge.

Apple, M. W. (2018). *The struggle for democracy in education: Lessons from social realities*. Routledge.

Apple, M. W., & Beane, J. A. (Eds.). (2007). *Democratic schools: Lessons in powerful education* (2nd ed.). Heinemann.

Arblaster, A. (1972). Education and ideology. In D. Rubinstein & C. Stoneman (Eds.), *Education for democracy* (2nd ed., pp. 34–40). Penguin Education.

Arendt, H. (1969). *Between past and future: Eight exercises in political thought*. The Viking Press.

Aronowitz, S. (2008). *Against schooling: Toward an education that matters*. Paradigm Publishers.

Aronowitz, S., & Giroux, H. (1987). *Education under siege: The conservative, liberal and radical debate over schooling*. Routledge & Keegan Paul Ltd.

Aronowitz, S., & Giroux, H. (1991). *Postmodern education: Politics, culture and social criticism*. University of Minnesota Press.

Ball, S. J., & Collette-Sabé, J. (2021). Against school: An epistemological critique. *Discourse: Studies in the Cultural Politics of Education*. https://doi.org/10.1080/01596306.2021.1947780

Barber, B. R. (1997). Public schooling: Education for democracy. In J. I. Goodlad & T. J. McMannon (Eds.), *The public purpose of education and schooling* (pp. 21–32). Jossey-Bass Publishers.

Bauman, Z. (2004). To hope is human. *Tikkun*, *19*(6), 64–67.

Beane, J. A., & Apple, M. W. (2007). The case for democratic schools. In M. W. Apple & J. A. Beane (Eds.), *Democratic schools: Lessons in powerful education* (2nd ed., pp. 1–29). Heinemann.

Biesta, G. (2010). *Good education in an age of measurement: Ethics, politics, democracy*. Routledge.

Biesta, G. (2013). *The beautiful risk of education*. Routledge.

Biesta, G. (2014). Learning in public places: Civic learning for the twenty-first century. In G. Biesta, M. De Bie, & Wildemeersch (Eds.), *Civic learning, democratic citizenship and the public sphere* (pp. 1–11). Springer.

Bingham, C., & Sidorkin, A. M. (Eds.). (2004). *No education without relation*. Peter Lang.

Bishop, M., & Vass, G. (2020). Talking about culturally responsive approaches to education: Teacher professional learning, Indigenous learners and the politics of schooling. *The Australian Journal of Indigenous Education*. https://doi.org/10.1017/jie.2020.30

Carr, P. R., & Thésée, G. (2019). *It's not education that scares me, it's the educators: Is there still hope for democracy in education, and education for democracy?* Myers Education Press.

Carr, W., & Hartnett, A. (1996). *Education and the struggle for democracy: The politics of educational ideas*. Open University Press.

Connell, R. W. (1993). *Schools and social justice*. Temple University Press.

Connell, R. W. (2012). Just education. *Journal of Education Policy*, 27(5), 681–683. https://doi.org/10.1080/02680939.2012.710022

Connell, R. W. (2013). The neoliberal cascade and education: An essay on the market agenda and its consequences. *Critical Studies in Education*, 54(2), 99–112. https://doi.org/10.1080/17508487.2013.776990

Counts, G. S. (1932). *Dare the school build a new social order?* The John Day Company.

Dewey, J. (1899). *The school and society: Being three lectures*. University of Chicago Press.

Dewey, J. (1902). *The child and the curriculum*. University of Chicago Press.

Dewey, J. (1916). *Democracy and education: An introduction to the philosophy of education*. The Macmillan Company.

Edwards-Groves, C., Kemmis, R. B., Hardy, I., & Ponte, P. (2010). Relational architectures: Recovering solidarity and agency as living practices in education. *Pedagogy, Culture & Society*, 18(1), 43–54. https://doi.org/10.1080/14681360903556814

Ferrara, A. (2014). *The democratic horizon: Hyperpluralism and the renewal of political liberalism*. Cambridge University Press.

Fielding, M. (2007). On the necessity of radical state education: Democracy and the common school. *Journal of Philosophy of Education*, 41(4), 539–557.

Fielding, M., & Moss, P. (2010). *Radical education and the common school: A democratic alternative*. Routledge.

Freire, P. (1972). *Pedagogy of the oppressed*. Penguin Books.

Gardels, N., & Berggruen, N. (2019). *Renovating democracy: Governing in the age of globalization and digital capitalism*. University of California Press.

Gay, G. (2015). The what, why, and how of culturally responsive teaching: International mandates, challenges, and opportunities. *Multicultural Education Review*, 7(3), 123–139. https://doi.org/10.1080/2005615X.2015.1072079

Giroux, H. A. (2003). Public pedagogy and the politics of resistance: Notes on a critical theory of educational struggle. *Educational Philosophy and Theory*, 35(1), 5–16. https://doi.org/10.1111/1469-5812.00002

Giroux, H. A. (2004). Public pedagogy and the politics of neoliberalism: Making the political more pedagogical. *Policy Futures in Education*, 2(3–4), 494–503. https://doi.org/10.2304/pfie.2004.2.3.5

Giroux, H. A. (2005). Cultural studies in dark times: Public pedagogy and the challenge of neoliberalism. *Fast Capitalism*, 1(2), 75–86. https://doi.org/10.32855/fcapital.200502.010

Giroux, H. A. (2009). *Youth in a suspect society: Democracy or disposability?* Palgrave Macmillan.

Giroux, H. A. (2010). Rethinking education as the practice of freedom: Paulo Freire and the promise of critical pedagogy. *Policy Futures in Education, 8*(6), 715–721.

Giroux, H. A. (2016). *Schooling and the struggle for public life: Democracy's promise and education's challenge* (2nd ed.). Routledge.

Goodlad, J. I. (1979). *What schools are for*. Phi Delta Kappa Educational Foundation.

Goodlad, J. I. (2011). Convergence. In R. Soder, J. I. Goodlad, & T. J. McMannon (Eds.), *Developing democratic character in the young* (pp. 1–25). Jossey-Bass.

Gutmann, A. (1999). *Democratic education*. Princeton University Press.

Heggart, K., & Kolber, S. (Eds.). (2022). *Empowering teachers and democratising schooling*. Springer.

Heimans, S., Singh, P., & Kwok, H. (2021). Pedagogic rights, public education and democracy. *European Educational Research Journal*. https://doi.org/10.1177/14749041211011920

Hickey, A., & Riddle, S. (2021). Relational pedagogy and the role of informality in renegotiating learning and teaching encounters. *Pedagogy, Culture & Society*. https://doi.org/10.1080/14681366.2021.1875261

Hickey, A., Riddle, S., Robinson, J., Down, B., Hattam, R., & Wrench, A. (2021). Relational pedagogy and the policy failure of contemporary Australian schooling: Activist teaching and pedagogically driven reform. *Journal of Educational Administration and History*. https://doi.org/10.1080/00220620.2021.1872508

Hickey, A., Riddle, S., Robinson, J., Hattam, R., Down, B., & Wrench, A. (2022). Relational pedagogy and democratic education. In S. Riddle, A. Heffernan, & D. Bright (Eds.), *New perspectives on education for democracy: Creative responses to local and global challenges* (pp. 200–212). Routledge.

Ladson-Billings, G. (1995). Toward a theory of culturally relevant pedagogy. *American Educational Research Journal, 32*(3), 465–491. https://doi.org/10.3102/00028312032003465

Ladson-Billings, G. (2014). Culturally relevant pedagogy 2.0: a.k.a. the remix. *Harvard Educational Review, 84*(1), 74–84. https://doi.org/10.17763/haer.84.1.p2rj131485484751

Ladson-Billings, G. (2021). I'm here for the hard re-set: Post pandemic pedagogy to preserve our culture. *Equity & Excellence in Education, 54*(1), 68–78. https://doi.org/10.1080/10665684.2020.1863883

Lewis, J. (2020, 30 July). Together, you can redeem the soul of our nation. *The New York Times*. https://www.nytimes.com/2020/07/30/opinion/john-lewis-civil-rights-america.html

Ljungblad, A. L. (2019). Pedagogical relational teachership (PeRT): A multi-relational perspective. *International Journal of Inclusive Education*. https://doi.org/10.1080/13603116.2019.1581280

McCarty, T., & Lee, T. (2014). Critical culturally sustaining/revitalizing pedagogy and Indigenous education sovereignty. *Harvard Educational Review, 84*(1), 101–124. https://doi.org/10.17763/haer.84.1.q83746nl5pj34216

McLaren, P., & Farahmandpur, R. (2005). *Teaching against global capitalism and the new imperialism: A critical pedagogy*. Rowman & Littlefield Publishers.

McMannon, T. J. (1997). Introduction: The changing purposes of education and schooling. In J. I. Goodlad & T. J. McMannon (Eds.), *The public purpose of education and schooling* (pp. 1–20). Jossey-Bass Publishers.

Mills, M., Riddle, S., McGregor, G., & Howell, A. (2021). Towards an understanding of curricular justice and democratic schooling. *Journal of Educational Administration and History*. https://doi.org/10.1080/00220620.2021.1977262

Monbiot, G. (2016). *How did we get into this mess? Politics, equality, nature*. Verso.

Morrison, A., Rigney, L.-I., Hattam, R., & Diplock, A. (2019). *Toward an Australian culturally responsive pedagogy: A narrative review of the literature.* https://apo.org.au/sites/default/files/resource-files/2019-08/apo-nid262951.pdf

Mouffe, C. (1993). *The return of the political.* Verso.

Mouffe, C. (1999). Deliberative democracy or agonistic pluralism? *Social Research, 66*(3), 745–758.

Mouffe, C. (2019). *For a left populism.* Verso.

Paris, D. (2012). Culturally sustaining pedagogy: A needed change in stance, terminology, and practice. *Educational Researcher, 41*(3), 93–97. https://doi.org/10.3102/0013189X12441244

Paris, D. (2021). Culturally sustaining pedagogies and our futures. *The Educational Forum, 85*(4), 364–376. https://doi.org/10.1080/00131725.2021.1957634

Rancière, J. (1991). *The ignorant schoolmaster: Five lessons in intellectual emancipation* (K. Ross, Trans.). Stanford University Press.

Rancière, J. (2006). *Hatred of democracy.* Verso.

Rancière, J. (2010). *Dissensus: On politics and aesthetics.* Continuum.

Riddle, S. (2019). Democracy and education in local–global contexts. *The International Education Journal: Comparative Perspectives, 18*(1), 1–6.

Riddle, S., & Apple, M. W. (Eds.). (2019). *Re-imagining education for democracy.* Routledge.

Riddle, S., & Cleaver, D. (2017). *Alternative schooling, social justice and marginalised students.* Palgrave Macmillan.

Riddle, S., Heffernan, A., & Bright, D. (Eds.). (2022a). *New perspectives on education for democracy: Creative responses to local and global challenges.* Routledge.

Riddle, S., Heffernan, A., & Bright, D. (2022b). On the need for a new democracy of education in a post-pandemic world. In S. Riddle, A. Heffernan, & D. Bright (Eds.), *New perspectives on education for democracy: Creative responses to local and global challenges* (pp. 3–8). Routledge.

Sant, E. (2021). *Political education in times of populism: Towards a radical democratic education.* Palgrave Macmillan.

Schostak, J. (2019). 'Towards a society of equals': Democracy, education, cooperation and the practice of radical inclusion. *International Journal of Inclusive Education, 23*(11), 1103–1115. https://doi.org/10.1080/13603116.2019.1629161

Schostak, J., & Goodson, I. (2020). *Democracy, education and research: The struggle for public life.* Routledge.

Schwab, K., & Malleret, T. (2020). *COVID-19: The great reset.* Forum Publishing.

Sidorkin, A. M. (2000). Toward a pedagogy of relation. *Faculty Publications, 17.* http://digitalcommons.ric.edu/facultypublications/17

Srnicek, N., & Williams, A. (2016). *Inventing the future: Postcapitalism and a world without work.* Verso.

Street, P. (2015). *They rule: The 1% vs. democracy.* Routledge.

Taylor, A. (2019). *Democracy may not exist, but we'll miss it when it's gone.* Verso.

Waldron, J. (2010). Arendt on the foundations of equality. In S. Benhabib (Ed.), *Politics in dark times: Encounters with Hannah Arendt* (pp. 17–39). Cambridge University Press.

Zembylas, M. (2020). The affective atmospheres of democratic education: Pedagogical and political implications for challenging right-wing populism. *Discourse: Studies in the Cultural Politics of Education.* https://doi.org/10.1080/01596306.2020.1858401

INDEX

Apple, M. 2–3, 23, 33, 47–48, 53, 110
Arendt, H. 6, 76–77, 123

Belarus 41
Biesta, G. 24, 100, 109, 120
Brexit 37, 42, 69

capitalism 7, 30, 47, 50, 64, 78, 86
civics education 17, 21, 53
civil disobedience 92–97
climate change 85–91, 108
Connell, R. W. 17, 60, 109, 116
Counts, G. 4, 30, 77, 111
COVID-19 see pandemic
crisis 6–7
curriculum 18, 20–23, 80

Dewey, J. 9, 23, 33, 100
Dorling, D. 12–13, 42

economic inequality *see* inequality
Extinction Rebellion 3, 32, 88

Facebook 67–68, 73
fascism 14, 38, 71
Freire, P. 112–113, 118

globalisation 5, 35, 93, 95, 102, 107
Giroux, H. 5, 12, 15, 47, 51, 61, 92, 115

inequality 12–13, 15, 30–31, 42, 65

LeGuin, U. 4
liberalism 2, 15, 30, 33–34, 37

McLaren, P. 13, 101
Monbiot, G. 14, 39, 43, 102
Mouffe, C. 7, 11, 34, 38, 46–47, 50, 52, 77–78, 101, 121–122
Myanmar 40–41

neo-conservatism 3, 18, 48, 100, 122
neofascism 5, 11, 25, 30, 37, 49
neoliberalism 5, 7, 11–12, 31, 43–49, 78, 92, 111
net zero emissions 90, 98

Occupy movement 93–94

pandemic 13, 59–66, 86–87, 108
pedagogy: critical pedagogy 115, 118; relational pedagogy 115–117
populism 14, 72–78
postmodernism 66–67
post-truth 51, 66, 70, 76, 78–79
progressive education 18
public education 25
public pedagogy 92

QAnon conspiracy 72

Rancière, J. 10, 34, 47, 50, 52, 117, 121
Riddle, S. 2–3, 16, 22, 44, 48, 110, 119

School Strike for Climate 3, 88, 95, 114
social inequality *see* inequality
social justice 22, 35, 53, 118
Syria 41

Thunberg, G. 95–96
Trump, Donald 38–39, 60, 69–72
Twitter 38, 70

United Kingdom 20, 37, 42–43, 69, 95
United States of America 20, 37, 38–40, 69

Printed in the United States
by Baker & Taylor Publisher Services